What Happened to
SANDRA?

Published in the UK in 2021
by Mcmenamin Publishers

Paperback   ISBN 978-1-7399195-0-4
eBook   ISBN 978-1-7399195-1-1

Cover design and typeset by SpiffingCovers

What Happened to
SANDRA?

The true story of the courage it took to bring her abusers to justice

SANDRA HARRISON

Prologue

This is a true story of a horrific paedophile ring that led to the murder of a young girl and a survivor to tell the story. I had to let the world know the truth, as it ate away inside me like venom from a poisonous snake. My family and friends knew a completely different person, as I was really a great actress on and off stage and still can be today. It is about a young, innocent child with a life of such horrendous abuse. This book is certainly not for the weak, or the faint of heart, and it is all true, not elaborated in any way. It's sad and cruel, but there is some humour amongst the story. I do hope you enjoy or, better still, identify with this book. This is my first written work called:

What Happened to Sandra?
Written by
Sandra Wilson Harrison McMenamin

Chapter One

It was the 3rd October 1961, and the cry of a newborn baby girl rang out in the Rankin Maternity Hospital while the mother struggled at death's door. A message got out to the father, who arrived at the hospital.

The doctor turned to him and said, "Your baby's fine, but the mother is dying." My father was handed me as this baby.

He said to the doctor, "What do I do with her?"

The doctor replied, "Do you not have another nine children, Mr. H?"

Mr. H replied, "I have worked at sea a lot. I have never changed a baby's nappy or even fed one." Just then my older sister, who was 13 years old, appeared. My father broke down in tears and said, "OK, Kathleen, I'm gonna need your help with this baby."

The mother was so ill they didn't think she would make it, so Mr. H and Kathleen took the child home to 4 Stafford Road in Greenock, Scotland. The mother survived but was kept in hospital for three months. Mr. H, at this time of his life, was becoming a Christian and, although he drank a lot of alcohol and was never there for the other nine children, went down on his knees and he thanked the Lord for giving him this baby girl, which he'd prayed for when his wife was pregnant because there were six boys, and he'd prayed knowing this would be the last chance for a baby to be a girl, because both parents were in their middle forties now and they had enough mouths to feed.

He said, "This baby shall be called Alexsandra Wilson Harrison," and he shortened my first name to Sandra. While at home, with the mother still in hospital, Mr. H (everyone called him Wee Johnny) did the best he could, obviously with help of Kathleen, and formed a bond with Sandra that he'd never had with any of the other kids.

Sandra was Johnny's pride and joy. Kathleen bonded so well with her she was like Sandra's mum rather than her sister. The neighbours all helped, and Wee Johnny was in his glory, celebrating with his Christian friends for his prayers being answered. Sadie, my biological mother, came out of hospital and tried to look after Sandra, but just a week after leaving hospital, she had a massive stroke and got rushed to Glasgow Infirmary for another four months. By this time I, Wee Sandra, would have been almost nine months old and because Kathleen was there as mother, so Sadie, the real mum, and myself, Sandra, never bonded.

They had very little money and struggled to buy food. Wee Johnny stayed home from the sea, drove buses and worked up on the Gryffe farms in Kilmacolm. I had three older sisters and six brothers. My two eldest sisters were married in Scotland; Ruby had a boy named Frankie then a son named Danny. Isabel had a daughter Linda then another daughter Shirley. Sandra, Linda and Frankie were roughly the same age, so I was an aunty when I was three years old. Well, three months old actually, as my mother and her two daughters were pregnant at the same time; my mother having her last child, me, and my two older sisters having their first child.

The first memory I have as a child is when I was three years old, and was still sleeping in a cot, waking up during the night crying and then talking to my imaginary friend who I'd named Mary Hopkins. My eldest sister, Ruby, decided to leave Greenock on a £10.00 discount fare to Australia when her second boy, Danny, was a baby. This was to get a better life, I was told, as there were good jobs, houses etc. She was gone eight months then wrote to my other two sisters to come out to Australia too, as it was a life beyond their dreams. So they did. Isabel had two girls at this time, Linda and Shirley, and with her husband Alex, they decided to adopt Kathleen, as she was only young, under 21, and she willingly left with them. I remember my father holding me in his arms, and I was screaming, sobbing so hard, as I wanted to go with them, as my bond with my sister Kathleen was so strong. Apparently, she wanted to take me, but my father wouldn't let me go, as I was his baby. So I was left feeling like an abandoned child at three years old.

I can't remember it but, my first traumatic experience was when I was two years old. A boy upstairs from us, as we lived in the bottom house of six apartments, stripped me naked and put me in an old, metal dustbin with hot ashes, put the lid on me and left me to die. Some of the girls in Stafford Road where playing at what they called 'wee housies', my sister Kathleen was playing too, and they decided to lift the bin lid to use it to play with. They got such a fright to see me, a two-year-old, blue and not breathing in the bin. They lifted me out. The local old woman's daughter was outside, as she lived next door, and she heard the girls shouting; luckily she was a nurse and resuscitated me back to life. I was told by my old mo, the woman that gave birth to me, that I was taken up to hospital right away, but there is no record of that to this very day, and apparently the police were involved but said because this boy was special needs they couldn't charge him. He was only slightly backwards, and had a clubbed foot, but was in Glenburn School for special needs. I do not remember this abuse, though my old mo, Sadie, kept telling me about it for years to come, she blamed that incident for all my behaviours as a child. I wasn't an unruly child. I was very quiet and always felt alone and different, although I had six big brothers.

My first memory of my sexual abuse was when I was four years old. I had measles, my eldest brother, John, was looking after me. He started to rub my vagina then told me to hold his penis. I was very sick and weak, but I did what I was told, as that's what special girls did and he said I was his. This abuse, from that instance, went on through my whole childhood. John would sexually abused me anally and make me touch him then give me money for it as a reward. Also at this time, the man who put me in the bin was sexually abusing me, then my two other older brothers started to abuse me; there was not one day or night I hadn't been abused by these men, all at different times and, as we had nothing, we were very poor, they would reward me with money, sweets and chocolate. Then all these other men started abusing me too, the neighbours in Stafford Road, John's friends that came to our house when on leave; I didn't realize until now, at the age of 57, that it was a massive paedophile ring, and they were all in this together and all knew each other. There were times I would be taken from the street playing and put into the back of a car, taken away to different places in Greenock, like the forest, the woods, the waterworks factory, shops and car garages, and abused as a child. I was threatened and told nobody would believe me if I said anything, or that I would get taken away never to be seen again. I got so used to all these men, including my brothers, sexually abusing me, it was a natural thing for me to do. This is all from the age of two years old until six years old. At one time, I was so sore down below, my old mo took me to the doctors, and he said it was because I was wearing nylon pants, and my old mo was told to get me cotton ones. I used to go and stay with my granny, Old Beanie she was called, and she was so good to me. She was deaf and couldn't speak properly, so by the age of five I knew sign language. I did get peace from my predators when I stayed with my granny, but she didn't keep well, so I couldn't go down to Duff Street, where she lived, as much as I would have liked to.

Thinking back, I was so used to being abused as a child it became normal. Now, I count 23 predators, although there were a lot more, I just don't know their names. I would like to say there was a leader. Well, I don't know if there was, it's just funny how they all knew each other, and my predators could tell me who had abused me and where it happened. In my early days, they called it 'interfering with' not paedophilia, and the ones who did it were called perverts.

I remember the abuse my pets all suffered. I had a tortoise called George, and one of my predators, named Alex, pulled the shell right off it, and beat it so badly with a hammer, while I was made to watch this. I was crying so much you'd think someone had ripped my heart out. He killed George my tortoise and made me bury what was left of him round the back green in Stafford Road.

While doing this, he would say, "Tell anybody I touched your bum or you touched my cock and this will happen to you," then he would make me touch him till he ejaculated. Afterwards, he would laugh and say to me, "Yer nothing but a clatty, wee bitch. Noo beat it," which means go away. I was eight at this time. I told my other brothers, but they just said that 'cause Alex was daft it was expected of him.

I would speak with my other brother, when I was five or six, his name was Harry. He used to ask what the predators did to me then tell me to do the same to him. I remember, in the toilet of this six-apartment building in Stafford Road, getting taken into it, with my two other brothers, Edward and Joseph, by Harry and he sexually abused us all. I remember when it was my turn to be abused by Harry, I was screaming, as my anus was getting probed like someone was sticking a very hot, hard instrument into my bum. He did stop, as I was screaming too much.

Then my brother Joseph said, "Leave my wee sister alone," and I was put out of the toilet – well, thrown out. I can't even imagine what my other two brothers Edward and Joseph went through, it was horrific.

Harry would come into my bedroom at night, and if I didn't let him touch me he would punch me in the arms and legs, right on the muscle, and say, "Wait till you see these bruises in the morning." So I had to let his abuse happen, otherwise he would punch me badly. My older brother Billy was in Australia at this time, and John, my other brother, would have been at sea, my father, Wee Johnny, would have been at work, and my old mo had a serious gambling problem, so she was at the bingo.

We didn't have any food in our house, so we

were always hungry. A local neighbour and her husband lived across the road from us, and he was also one of my predators. She worked in a butcher's and would send my old mo over big pieces of meat, mince, chicken, stew and steak, so she was well liked for helping the family with food, but her husband was one of the ring. He started on me at five years old. He had a car and he would lift me from the streets, while I was playing with my wee pals, and take me to the forest, the waterworks and places underground, places with big tunnels that cleansed dirty into clean water. No one knew where these places were, he called them secret places only special children were taken to, and sexually abused me there. He worked for the corporation at the town council, now known as Inverclyde District Council, and he held the keys to all these secret places. One I really remember was in Wemyss Bay, on a private road. You went down steps to a doorway, which was very near the beach, it was a small door with a yellow sign on it, reading 'Keep Out, High Voltage, Dangerous', but inside this place was massive. It had all these pumps and big tanks and pools, like rounds swimming pools, and it would have been another waterworks. This place had a separate room, I remember it well as I was told to take off all my clothes and, naked, he would lift me up on to this steel table and proceed to abuse me. I would just lie there, with tears rolling down the side of my face, hoping he would ejaculate, as then I knew it was over.

He would say, "You're such a good, wee girl, Sandra. We all love you more than any wain in Greenock." Wain is another word for child in their early years. He'd then give me £5.00, sometimes £10.00, then drive back to Stafford Road and tell me to get out of the car, and if any adult asked I was to say I was just away on a wee run with him to the garage. It so happened that, when I was told to leave the car, my old mo would be at the window of my home in 4 Stafford Road watching this; she knew all along. During my abuse with this man, he used to ask me to get as many of my wee pals involved with this and I would get paid more, but I never let him, or any other predators, get to some of my pals, as I didn't like it. Why would I let them go through something I knew was wrong?

So I would just say, "No, just take me instead."

It was awful, this abuse, as his daughter was my best friend, and I was too scared to tell her what her sick dad was doing to me and other children he would pick up. Also, her mother practically put food on our table, especially when she moved jobs to a food store. My old mo would have nothing bad to say about her or him.

I got to six and I hated being abused, so I told my old mo that my brothers and other men were abusing me. She slapped me on the face and called me a little liar. That's when I did become a liar; even my own mother didn't believe me.

I did tell one of our neighbours, and she said, "Just keep away from these people," but as a child, they would always find me, even come and take me from primary school and then drop me back when they could.

I was so shy and insecure as a child, it was so unreal, all I wanted to do was sing and play theatre parts. This kept my mind off the horrific abuse I was struggling with as a child, but they, if nothing else, all made me feel wanted, apart from my old mo; she hated me. I could feel how evil she was, especially when she hit me. My father knew nothing of my abuse. I was so scared to tell anyone, as I always thought it was my fault, and I was also told by my predators that I asked for this. It now makes me wonder why my mother would take the money they gave me and then call me a good girl. I so loved this, as I always wanted her attention. The only human touch I remember, with my mother, was when she was taking the lice from my head. I still remember the noise of them cracking. I always had long hair, as a child, and I always caught lice, but feeling my old mo's hands going through my hair was great. She never called my name or lifted me up affectionately, maybe in front of people she would pretend to love me, but I knew this was all false.

I do remember the fun times as a child. I invented an imaginary friend called Mary Hopkins, and I remember cutting my hair and saying Mary Hopkins did it. I also had loads of dolls, from nearly every country in the world, brought back from sea by John. I loved all my dolls. My brothers Joseph, Vincent and Edward were very close to me. Vincent regularly annoyed me because he was jealous of the attention my dad, Edward and Joseph gave me, but also

Vincent didn't know about my abuse, so he hated me getting all this money, sweets and extra toys. He used to hit me a lot that once he punched me so much my legs were covered in bruises. I do remember Vincent telling me to stand against a wall, he had made a bow and arrow from old wood and string, and he would proceed to fire arrows at me saying he was going to be a circus act. He was supposed to miss me, but he didn't. They caught my legs, my arms and hit my nose, to the extent of it bleeding for ages. He did panic, as it wouldn't stop.

It was only me and Vincent in the house, my father was always working, and my old mo was cleaning people's houses for money. The rich people we called them, as they lived in big houses down The Esplanade in Greenock. Sometimes she would take me, Joseph and Vincent with her. We would play in their big, lovely gardens while my old mo cleaned the house. Sometimes she would call us in to help clean and scrub wooden floors or wash and dry dishes. We also had a rota in the house for our chores it was written on a piece of paper and stuck to our bedroom doors. By the age of seven I got my own room, but before this I was in the same room as my old mo and my dad. I can remember them going out to the LMA club and my brothers looking after me. Sometimes things with my abuse would calm down, especially when John was at sea. Billy had gone to Australia and Harry was there too, so at one time in my life as a child I had three sisters and two brothers in Australia and one at sea. Although, at times, John's seaman friends would pop in for a visit, and they always brought alcohol from abroad with cigarettes. My dad, being a heavy drinker and smoker, welcomed these men in, and my old mo would cook for them. They would end up staying with us, and some of them – not them all – would come into my bedroom at night.

I do remember one man, stinking of whisky, coming into my bedroom, climbing into my bed, then saying to me that this was OK. John told them to do this, he'd say, and he'd also tell me about the toys I'd be getting when John came home. I got so used to this happening to me it became acceptable. Every night, before I fell asleep, I would say my prayers. I would kneel down in front of this big, black iron crucifix with

Jesus on it and pray I would be able to sleep all night without anyone coming into my room, and then I would ask Jesus to bless everyone in my family and also the sick. I never was taught I could pray for myself until I was 15.

I remember I had a Silver Cross dolls' pram, and my special doll Jenny was always in it. One day, I woke up with boys laughing and shouting; it was my three brothers. They had made a bogie, which was a wooden box with wheels, and were rolling it down Stafford Road. I stood at the window and laughed, as they were having great fun. I went out to play with them, and then I realized they had stripped my pram and used the wheels for the bogie. I was crying, but as soon as they put me in the bogie, Edward always steered it with a rope, I was loved it and didn't mind them using my pram 'cause this was so much fun.

I was trying to come up with lots of ideas to make more friends, so I opened up a dolls' hospital. All the children would bring their broken dolls, I would keep them overnight, get my brother Edward to fix them, as Edward was always fixing things, and give them back to their owner the following day. Once, my friend Linda came in with her doll, which was called a Tiny Tears doll, with her arm off. Edward fixed this right away, but I'd never had a Tiny Tears doll and love this one. I told her that her doll's arm was so badly broken she would have to leave her in my dolls' hospital for days; this was only so I could play with her. Then one day, Linda caught me playing around the back green with her Tiny Tears doll all fixed, and I had to give her it back.

My three brothers who were very close to me, and apart from Vincent's antagonizing, I loved them so much. They didn't abuse me and we never spoke about our abuse, it was such a big secret. We made our own fun as kids. I became popular as a child, as I would go out and make friends with anyone. Even if they were new to the street, I was always first at the door asking them to come out and play. Once, a big family moved into the street. One of their girls was a little person, we called them dwarfs then, I thought she was a similar age to me and went up to ask her to come out and play. She shut her door in my face. All my other friends were laughing, as they knew she was a dwarf, they just didn't tell me. I did say sorry afterwards.

My friends and I used to play wee shops, using grass as chips, leaves as fish and small stones as pickled onions. This was great, and I seemed to always be the shopkeeper. We would also make up little plays, and I would sing. I loved singing. My dad taught me my keys when I was just three, and I would always be the lead singer. In our six-bedroom house we had a piano, which was given free to my dad from one of the rich people my old mo worked for, so the family were very musical. I used to sing at all the parties I was invited to, and also at all the drunken parties that were in my home nearly every weekend. I loved this attention, and they would put me on the table, I'd sing and they'd all clap their hands. This was the only time in my young childhood that I felt wanted. These drunken parties would get more regular, and then they would all start fighting; a houseful of people, family and friends, singing one minute then fighting the next. I remember my dad played a saw, he would bend it, hit it and get a tune from it, my brother John would play the spoons, someone would be making a tune from an old washboard – the only real instrument we had was the piano – I would sing, and then someone would say the wrong word and all hell would break out; the saw getting used now as a weapon. My old mo would run out of the house in fear. I would hide with my dolls under the bed and hold my ears. I was so, so scared that someone would find me, then the police would come, people would get taken away and then everything was silent. Many a time, I would crawl out from under the bed to see blood spurted all over the walls, the house smashed up and only me there, perhaps sometimes a couple of drunks asleep on the chairs. I would just go into my room and climb into bed. I was so aware of no one coming in to check I was OK, I would cry myself to sleep.

I was brought up Roman Catholic. Very strict, hostile nuns taught me – that's what I called them. It was more like an army camp than a school. Punishment was horrific, humiliating and scary. If you struggled to read out in class, you would get shouted at, sent to the dunce's corner, which was a corner of the classroom where the other pupils would make fun of you and the teacher would totally ignore you, and you were also kept in at playtime which was your break outside with your friends. As I was bullied by a boy and a girl in school, I wasn't too bothered about being in the corner which actually was quite a lot. Primary school was so hard for me as I was dyslexic, but I just got called stupid and was bullied for that too, plus the teacher would humiliate me by calling me by my second name and letting the class know I couldn't read or write properly. Every morning, one of the class was picked to say morning prayers, and you said the first part of the Hail Mary prayer then the rest of the class would join in on the second part. I hated it when this was my turn say, as I always stumbled over my words. Once, I got so scared about not remembering the first part of the Hail Mary, the teacher made all the class stay silent.

"Silence!" she shouted. "Not a peep until Harrison," (again my second name) she'd say, "remembers the Hail Mary." I actually peed my pants, got pulled by my shirt out of the class and down to the nurse station to get a bawling and given a pair of brown shorts to wear which were called the brown peed shorts, with no pants. My skirt and pants were put in a bag and I was told to put them in my desk, our desks opened up you see, and then I took them home with a note for my parents.

When this happened, my old mo battered me and told me, "You pished yerself in school. Noo they'll all be talking about us."

I got sent to my room, crying again, fell asleep, only to get woken by one of my older brothers lying in bed beside me, whispering in my ear, "It's OK, I'm here now," then I got sexually abused and told that was love. Every other way I was treated was evil, I hated it, but the more I said no the more angry my predators would get.

I do remember getting angry at one point and saying, "I'm gonna tell somebody what you're doing to me," then I would get punched, never on my face, always on my legs, stomach or arms. I was always bruised where people couldn't see. By the age of seven, my back bottom used to bleed a lot, as they all tried so hard to have anal sex with me. As I was very small and frail, I remember the pain being so bad it would knock me out. My vagina was never penetrated as a child. When I got older, I thought this was so they wouldn't get me pregnant or get caught if I ever got examined by a doctor down below, but after my old mo had taken me to the doctor when I was three and told my vagina was so scarred and red because of wearing nylon pants, I was never taken back to the doctor. I didn't even start going regularly to the doctors until I was 14 years old, as I know now that my old mo didn't want anyone to know I was getting sexually abused, and yes, she knew. I will never forget that slap when I was six and was called a liar, and then the following year getting a communion dress and taking my first communion. I wasn't surprised that none of my family were there to see me though all of my friends' parents were there. After my communion, with my borrowed dress from Linda next door who'd taken hers the year before, my old mo was in the house with all, or most, of my predators, all waiting to see Wee Sandra with her nice white dress on, like a wee bride, then she sent me round people's front doors to get money, as this was supposed to be my special day, because all my sins had been forgiven and I had received Jesus Christ's body into my soul. It didn't feel like that to me, as my mother knew who would give me money for letting them abuse me, and she sent me specifically to their houses. When I got home, she took the money, said I'd been a very good girl and smiled at me with 'the smile'. I felt good getting it. It only seemed to happen when my mother was getting money. Money was her god. It upsets me now, as an adult, to think your own mother could actually prostitute her only daughter out, as my sisters had a different mum, but this became normality.

I also used to go carol-singing. I asked my friends to come with me, as I loved singing. We would knock on any door and as soon as it opened burst into 'Silent Night' or 'Away in a Manger', and in our hands we held an empty bean tin saying on it 'For the Sisters of the Poor'. We would make good money, as we walked down to The Esplanade, because we knew that's where the rich people stayed. This would be from November till 24th December every year. Then I had a paper round delivering a local paper to houses over two or three miles from my own home. After that I had a job going round clearing people's paths of snow with a shovel bigger than me. I was always trying my best to make money for my old mo rather than getting it for sexual abuse, as when that happened the money felt dirty and I would feel dirty, guilty, scared and ashamed. It was a better feeling when my feet and hands were frozen from clearing the snowy paths or going to shops for people. I always wanted to give my old mo money 'cause then I was a good girl, every other time I was a cheeky, dirty, wee bitch and was slapped and battered at times to a pulp.

I would run away a lot as a child, and God must have been looking out for me, as someone would find me up the hill, or in the old farm up the back from our house, and take me home. No one in the house would even know I was gone, my dad was at work and mother, the old mo, was never in.

I do remember, as a child, I'd hate it when I saw my old mo getting a new brooch with a pin in it. She loved getting these as presents, as she used to stick the pin in my arm or leg and say it's good luck to do that to someone when you get a new brooch. She never did this to the boys in the house, just me.

It was sore too and always drew blood, then she'd tell me to lick the blood, as it was good for me, and told me, "Do not say anything to yer feather [that's what we called my dad] about this."

Then there were times in church, and in the house, where we would light candles for the dead. This now makes me think my mother was definitely a black witch. She also used to read people's tea leaves, and she always said she could read the future. My dad did not know any of this.

I couldn't tell anyone as my mo would say, "As soon as you tell secrets in the home you will get punished by God, and when you die you'll get put into the fires of hell." What went on in the family home stayed in the family home.

My father didn't know the half of my torture and abuse. I was his wee girl, and he loved me so much. I trusted him more than anyone in my life.

He would always say, "If anyone hurt my Wee Sandra I would kill them," and that's what stopped me telling my dad, as I didn't want anyone killed; I didn't want my dad to go to jail. Plus, I was brainwashed into thinking I was at fault and no one would believe me. As well as this, I was scared they would kill me and bury me up the hill, as that's what some of my predators would say to me if I told anyone, or I was threatened I'd get pushed under a train by one of my predators while he was abusing me in the woods behind the hospital where the railway line was. The day he took me into the woods, it was as if he'd planned that a train would be coming. Trains were very noisy in the sixties, and I was holding on to the railway fence, letting him touch me, as the train passed. I remember holding on so hard to this metal fence that my hands were all sore. I would, at this time, be eight or nine years old. This was a boy, a family friend, who was supposed to be looking after me. I now know this is not true, as I looked after myself.

I wasn't the cleanest of wee girls and was always dressed in some sort of rags my old mo would make for me. I never got any new clothes. She used to knit me things like ponchos, cardigans and jumpers and that was only because one of the neighbours worked in the old wool factory and got my mo free wool, anything else was from a rag store or was given to me by neighbours. I used to try and wash myself, and I remember having to use a stool to get to the sink, while the soap was the green Fairy household soap you washed your clothes with. As I only had cold water, I still couldn't get the dirt from my hands and nails. I used to bite my nails, as it was the only way I could get them clean.

I remember my dad getting a job in the shipyards cleaning the showers, so I asked if I could go with him to the showers to get washed. He said yes, as long as I wore a bathing suit, so I brought along my wee pal Anne, and we danced around the showers in our bathing suits for hours. I felt clean for days after that, as no one had showers in their house then. We didn't have computers, mobiles or all the electronic things you get today, this sort of thing was only seen in James Bond films.

I also remember getting our first colour television. I was around 11 then, maybe 10. I was amazed, as when I was allowed to watch TV before it was black and white, the signal was awful and it used to stop all the time.

When I became nine or 10 I remember my old mo saying, "Your brother Billy is coming home from Australia today." So we all had to clean the house, and we were all very excited to meet this brother I never knew, as he was shipped to Australia at the age of 14, because he was an unruly child and so my old mo had sent him away. I watched from the window of 4 Stafford Road with such excitement.

When I saw this tall, thin, dark, red-haired guy getting out of a taxi I was shouting, "It's Billy! Our Billy is home from Australia." I was desperate to hear all the stories about Australia, about its wildlife and my sisters, as by this time I'd forgotten what they looked like. Well Billy came in, dumped his suitcase down and said hello to us all. Joseph, Vincent and Edward, mo and feather (Dad) were all there. I can't remember if he gave us gifts, but I know for certain he had lots of alcohol, cigarettes and tobacco.

From that first day back the house just got 100% worse, as the fighting got worse. Billy was a bully, not the big, protective brother I was expecting from Australia. He used to batter Vincent, Joseph and Edward all the time, and with me he would shout and come into my bedroom at night just to scare me. He tortured my animals, never my dogs, just my cats, rabbits, pet mice or hamster. My cat was terrified of him. He would kick it so hard it would squeal and jump out of the window. Every cat I had he would torture, and then it would go missing. We had guns in the house, and he used to shoot the little robins that landed in our back garden and laugh, making me watch.

Sexual abuse with Billy didn't start until I was 14, before that I was terrified of this man, as I watched him kill a wee lamb he stole from the hill, shoot wee robins and kill and torture my cats, rabbits and pet mice. He was evil. All the other five boys were scared of this man, he was a complete psychopath. Even the oldest one, John, feared him. My father never trusted him, and said he was sleekit. He also had affairs with married women, he was very much a woman's man, and had a few girlfriends at the same time. He also has a few children now that don't know that he's their father.

Everyone feared Billy; he was a fighter, a bully and a liberty-taker. My first recollection of grooming by Billy was when he used to teach me how to play cards, a game he called scabby queen using pornographic cards. I remember asking him why didn't we play with normal cards, as they all did in the house at weekends when they had big poker schools. He said that this was our secret. Then the pornographic books got introduced to me. By this time, I would be nine or 10 and was coming in from school finding books on my bed under my pillow. I had my own room at this time. I remember being curious, as children are, opening them up to find human beings having sex with animals. I remember feeling sick and telling either Joseph, Vincent or Edward what I'd found, I'm pretty sure it was Joseph, only to hear later that night Joseph getting battered, punched and kicked by Billy for telling on him to my dad. Joseph took a lot of beatings from Billy, John and Harry.

I used to scream, banging on the room door, "Leave my brother alone." Joseph and I were so close. We knew Billy would torture our animals, so we used to hide them outside in a wee hut round the back of the house so he couldn't get them.

Then one night, my mo and feather were out all night, and Billy told me, "We are watching a Disney movie in the front room again tonight, and you should come in and watch it."

The room was called the big back room

and had a reel-to-reel projector with a big, white screen and stools all around, just like the cinemas. I heard all the boys come in laughing and the neighbours, but that was when I saw all my predators in one room together. I was told to sit at the front and the film would start. The lights went out and, to my shock, it was pure, hardcore porn that John had brought back from sea. I had to sit till the end of the film while, at different times, some man would come and sit beside me and touch my privates as well as play with themselves. I hated it.

I was too scared to move, as they would say, "Don't speak, just sit there and watch the film. It will be finished soon." There was more than one. It was as if they were taking turns to interfere with me. At the end of film, they were all laughing and clapping.

I ran into my room, feeling dirty and ashamed, when John came in and said, "You did good in there. Here's some money." The next day, I took local girls and boys to the shops and bought them sweets so they'd play with me, as I never had a lot of friends. I had to look for friends, but I was always scared to take them into my house, and I didn't want them to know what I had been going through.

Again, I told my mo that men were coming into my room at night and doing stuff to me, but I was told again that I was a liar, then I told my dad the boys were watching films in the room. One night, he had come in early from work, which was just before they came for me to come and watch. Joseph, Vincent and Edward used to get thrown out of the house when this was going on. Well, that specific night, my father went into the room and cleared the lot of them out, smashing up everything in the room. I heard screaming and fighting then the usual police coming.

I remember when it all went quiet, when the house was still, my dad saying, "Where is that wain of mine?"

My old mo screamed, "Never mind her, where's my boys?" Then she left.

I came out of room and my dad said, "There you are, hen. You OK? I'm just gonna go across the street to my friend's and you're coming with me." I always felt safe in that house, as my dad and his mate would have a drink while me and my pal Anne would play with our Miss World model dolls and have fun. This was during the school holidays, and I remember my dad saying to me that we were going on holiday to Hamilton, to my Uncle John's, who was my mother's brother and who I loved dearly. My dad said it would get me away from that sick house, so off we went. My dad wanted me to stay up there with my cousins because he knew I would get treated better, so I did for six weeks, until my old mo made me come home, back to Stafford Road, to get punched, battered, terrified and sexually abused. I hated it; I always wanted to be someone else.

During all this, I still managed to sing and get all the lead parts in my school plays. I loved the stage, and I loved being a different character, it took me out of myself, and when I sang people loved it. I loved to see their faces smiling and them clapping. I loved all the attention. I know now that being on stage was my coping mechanism, and I forgot all about my life of hell when I was entertaining others. My father was so proud of me.

I remember Billy waking me up at night touching my privates, me trying to move away from him, and then trying to pretend to be sleeping 'cause I feared him so much. Funny thing, the following morning he was a completely different brother, telling me he'd never hit me again and he was my protector, and if John or any of the others touched me he'd batter them. He was so nice that I was roped right into his sick, beastly way, and all his fighting and animal abuse was part of my grooming process. So if I didn't let him touch me on my bottom he would be nice to me, and I would then become his favourite girl.

John, at this time, was going out with a girl, Cathy, who was lovely and really didn't know he was a paedophile. She brought a girl into 4 Stafford Road to meet my brother Edward, who was the same age as him, like for a blind date, they were both 16, but as soon as Billy clapped eyes on her he took her. Her name was Sandra, and she also came from a big family. She fell pregnant, and they both got married, so Sandra became Sandra Harrison, the same name as me. Sandra was a lovely girl, so innocent. She became Billy's punching bag for years. I used to see this girl beaten to a pulp so badly that she was hospitalized. Sandra gave birth to a daughter who she loved so much. Billy just drank alcohol and battered her. She never worked, after having her daughter as, being a control freak, he wouldn't let her, and so Sandra just got on with being a mother to Mary.

My abuse started a lot with Billy around this time, as I was starting to get boobs, and he was happy enough to tell me I needed a bra, as well as brushing past me in an inappropriate way. Billy was a bully, he bullied my other brothers, and he was also an alcoholic. I had a cat who I love dearly. Billy used to hit my cat a lot, and it was terrified of him. Once, after he had battered Sandra and I'd tried to stick up for her, he attacked me then threw my wee Cheety Face, as I called my cat, against the garage door and broke its ribs. All its fur was falling off that badly, and the vet told me the cat was so nervous he may have to put it to sleep. He didn't have to, Billy made sure my cat was to have a horrendous death. He didn't tell me what he did to wee Cheety Face, and I do not wish to know the torture he put him through.

At this time, he was still constantly commenting on my body transforming into a young teenager. Sandra fell pregnant again and gave birth to a son, Paul. Just as she had her baby, her father died. I felt so sorry for her. Billy didn't have any notion of grief in his body, but his wife was so sad.

I used to babysit a lot and look after Mary and Paul. I loved the kids so much, and I took them for outings often. Once we went to Glasgow, and I was on the train with two kids. The woman sitting across from me thought I was their mother. I was 15, so I would have been a very young mother. I just laughed it off.

Then the woman said to Mary, who was only three, "Did you have a nice day with Mummy today?"

Instead of Mary saying this is my auntie, Mary said, "Yes, my mummy and my wee brother had a great time," so I just let it go. Mary kept calling me Mummy all day after that, but I just let that go as well.

As Paul couldn't speak, he used to just point at things if he wanted anything, but Mary was, as we called it, a wee bletherer, a wee granny cut down. She was such a funny, wee girl, and she reminded me of myself at her age. I loved them kids. Sandra asked me to be Paul's godmother. I was 15 years old, but I was very happy to do this.

The christening took place in St. Laurence's Catholic Church, then after that we went up to Sandra and Billy's, who now had a house in Clydeview Road, Greenock, part of what we called the Strone area of Greenock. It was tenement buildings and quite a violent street. Every weekend Sandra and Billy would go out, or drink in the house, and we'd watch the people fighting in the street, which used to scare me somewhat. I'd then have a bed made up on the floor of the room where Billy and Sandra slept. Many a night, I would feel Billy's hand under my cover, touching me inappropriately. I remember telling Sandra, and she said Billy thought I was her that's why he did it. I used to stay with them a lot, as I couldn't stand the abuse at 4 Stafford Road, but this abuse was happening in Clydeview Road now. I felt that everywhere I went, or stayed, I would get abused. As this had been going on all my life, I began to just accept it and, at times, prayed for it to stop, as this was another brother abusing me. When I asked him about this once, I was full of wine, he told me he did it because I enjoyed it, and it was better than what John did.

I ended up moving out, back to my old mo's

house again, as I did not like the abuse from Billy. I couldn't trust falling asleep beside him. Even on his couch, I would wake up with him lying next to me saying I was his wee sister and he would kill anyone else who did this to me, as if it made me feel better. He must have told John what he was doing, as John could tell me everything Billy did, so they were in on it together.

I look now at my grandkids and wonder how they could have taken away my childhood innocence, and this pains me so much, but I'm just overprotective with them, which is not a bad thing, as I would dread the thought of anyone abusing my grandkids, and I will do the best I can as a nana to make sure this never happens. I have four girls and a boy, grandchildren to my son and daughter.

Going further along in my journey of life, I met Cush, who was to become my first husband. We drank the same type of wine, called El Dorado, and both of us put Irn-Bru, the Scottish National drink, in it and that was the common denominator between us. We both lived our lives alcoholically and tried to play wee, happy families. I couldn't drink alcohol when I was pregnant, so I was a very unhappy pregnant bride. I got married in white, which was frowned upon by my old mo 'cause I was pregnant before marriage, which was a massive sin in the Catholic Church, so we got married. I was three months pregnant and very, very sick morning, noon and night.

After our wedding, Cush's sister Liz gave us her house in Dumbarton for our wedding night. At that time, it was traditional to carry the bride over the threshold of the house to the bedroom with you. Cush was so drunk, I had to carry him in. I was still very unhappy, because I couldn't join in with the drinking party, as my baby Charlene rejected it, although this didn't stop me trying to drink alcohol. You see, alcohol took all my fears away and had helped me deal with life as a victim, and it was also a great coping medicine, it would block out all of my abuse.

Cush and I moved into a small one-bedroom flat in Inverkip, a little village in Scotland, where the last British witch was burned at Bridgend, apparently, and on Christmas Eve of 1983, I woke up with my bed soaking wet. I started to hit Cush with the pillow and called him every name under the sun, thinking he'd wet the bed, to jump out of bed and realize it was me; my waters had broken.

I started crying, waking him up out of a drunken sleep, screaming, "The baby's coming! Hurry up. Phone an ambulance. I thought you'd peed the bed, but it was me. I'm sorry." I've never seen anyone sober up so quickly in all my life. So he ran down to the village to phone box, as we didn't have mobiles then or even a house phone, just a one-bedroom flat with a mortgage. You see, Cush had a good job in IBM, and I worked in the entertainment industry employed by Greenock Council, so we got a small mortgage and bought this little house for £15,000.

I was on maternity leave when my daughter was born, so off to the Rankin Hospital I went, in the ambulance. Well Cush also phoned and told my dad, as the ambulance would have to pass my old mo's house, and if he wanted to come up to the hospital I would love that. I loved my dad so much, I wanted him there. I wasn't really bothered about my mo, Sadie, but I wanted my dad with me. He was the only man in my life who never abused me sexually, and if he'd known my three older brothers had been doing it, and another 20 people, he would be in jail, because he would have killed them, as I was his baby girl. My dad was older then too, so I couldn't tell him, it would have hurt him so much 'cause he loved me unconditionally.

So me and Cush were in the ambulance getting blue-lighted up to Rankin Maternity Hospital and we passed my old mo's house. My dad saw the ambulance, jumped in my older brother John's pickup truck, which was flashing an orange light, and followed the ambulance to the waiting nurses and midwives who were laughing hilariously at all this. Well, it was funny when I remember it now.

So in I go. I already knew some of the midwives, as a couple stayed in the village, and I also had been admitted when I was pregnant with my daughter at eight weeks and had lost a fetus. Now I knew this was my daughter, a twin, because when I was eight weeks my brother Joseph had had to call Dr. Martin as an emergency – he had huge eyebrows and liked a good tipple too, as he came to my old mo's house.

He said on the phone to my brother Joseph, "Make sure she passes everything out into a basin so we can check she's had a miscarriage." Well I did, but when I got to hospital then, in early pregnancy, they were going to take me straight to theatre for a D and C they called it.

I said to Joseph, "I still feel there's a baby inside me."

Joseph said, "Can you feel life in your belly, Sandra?" I said yes, so Joseph demanded a scan to be set up and, lo and behold, my baby was still there inside but the other fetus was gone.

So now I'm in hospital on Christmas Eve, and I had to get another scan, as this new doctor could feel two lumps, because Charlene was lying in the second twin position, which was also proof that I'd lost a baby while carrying one to the end. Charlene was also premature, so I ended up getting a C-section under general emergency anaesthetic.

I just remember getting put to sleep, having a weird dream about the devil and John Harrison, and being scared, until I heard a voice say, "Sandra, don't be afraid. The devil's a fool." Then I came to in a ward of four patients and was handed a picture of my baby.

"You had a baby girl," the nurse told me.

Cush, my old mo and my dad saw Charlene before I did, as my blood had dropped dramatically and I had to have five pints of blood pumped into me which was the sorest thing ever. The blood was too thick for my veins, and they couldn't get it through my system properly, so they had to put it straight into a main artery in the middle of my arm to get it in. As Christmas Day came, I was on a blood drip, and Cush was out celebrating his first child, getting pissed as a fart with his father. Santa Claus came in to my ward and handed me my daughter; it was the best Christmas I had ever had in my whole life.

I got moved to a room on its own, as I was very sore with the blood drip. They gave me painkillers to settle the pain, but it was awful and it didn't help that I wanted to breastfeed my baby. I told the nurse that her name was Charlene, and they put her wee name band on. I would talk to this baby telling her, well promising her, that she would never have the terrible life I had. I got so overprotective with my daughter, but I've since found out that I was triggering terribly. I thought every male who looked at my daughter would want to take her away and abuse her. I was very,

very ill during this terrible thinking. The doctor, my family doctor who knew me since I was a child, diagnosed me with postnatal depression.

My daughter was pure blonde. She so reminded me of Anne, my childhood friend. We used to get together every Saturday night. As her granda brought Anne up, my wee father and he were best drinking buddies, so they would sit in the living room with a roaring hot, coal fire with Anne's cat, Lucky, which sort of lived forever. This cat used to sit on the fireplace like an ornament, and this used to amaze me. I loved Lucky. She was pure black with green eyes. My pal Anne was a few years younger than me. We played with our Miss World dolls and at dress-up and had a great time, while my father and Anne's granda, used to sit, drink wine and talk about the war.

I was around eight then, and I always had a wee job, paper rounds or cleaning snow from paths for people in the winter. The money I made went straight to my old mo, Sadie, for her housekeeping, and then I came up with another plan. I was always trying to raise money, as I got such attention from my old mo, and she was so nice to me when I was giving her money. That was the only time this woman was nice to me, when I was handing in money. I was just a wee child when I gave money into the house, so my new plan was carol-singing. I would wash out an empty tin, and go across the street for Anne. We would start at the end of November every year. We'd knock on someone's door and when they answered it we would break into Christmas hymns, then end with, "We wish you a merry Christmas and a happy new year." The people were always nice to us and put money in our tin when we'd finished, then we'd split the rest. Anne always got to keep her own money, but mine went into the family home.

We had so much fun doing this, and I loved singing. My father taught me my scales and keys when I was only three, and I always had loads of confidence. My father was so proud of me, and he never put me down, he always kept me up. I loved him so, so much. I do think now that my old mo was jealous of how close my dad and I were.

So there's me and Anne, snow all around us, welly boots, gloves and coats, every November and December we'd go and make money carol-singing. We used to make a lot, and sometimes we would give it to the Little Sisters of the Poor, a nun-run residential home for the sick and elderly. I didn't tell my old mo when I handed the cash over to the nuns, as she would have belted me and told me charity begins at home.

One of my predators must have been watching how close wee Anne and I were. He asked me to bring Anne up to the house with me, and she would also get paid for doing sexual stuff to him like playing with his penis and letting him touch us. I told him no, as I didn't want that to happen to Anne, 'cause I didn't like it one bit, and it scared me to even think another child would be made to do all these horrific, sexual things to another adult.

So I'd said, "No, take me instead, not Anne."

My predator said to me, "What a good, loyal friend you are, but I will get her myself if you don't bring her to me." I was scared for Anne, and I told her to keep well away from him. He was a family friend and always got hold of me.

He had a car, so used to huckle (remove) me from the street where I was playing what we called peevers or beds, similar to hopscotch or elastics, which was a game of jumping over tied up elastic bands which were held out to each side with another child.

This one predator would stop in his car and huckle me or say, "Sandra, you're coming with me on a run. I'm looking after you for an hour."

I would look up to see my old mo's face at the window, watching me getting taken away. She knew I'd come back with money, so she let this happen often.

Sometimes wee Anne would be playing with us too, and I remember Anne saying, "Where's you going, Sandra?"

I'd say, "I will be back soon," and I would go in the car.

Sometimes there were two men in the car. I would get taken to various places and abused, given money, then dropped back off at the street afterwards to play with my friends, some of who had gone home by this time. I would go up to 4 Stafford Road, try and wash what they called my smelly, wee fanny, which was sore from the rubbing of their penis all around it and was still smelling of their sperm.

I would hear my old mo shouting, "Sandra, get in here. I need to look at yer heid." That was the only human touch I remembered from my mo. She would tug at my long hair with a steel comb and remove all the lice and nits I had. I always remember the cracking noise it made when she killed them with her nail.

She'd say, "Yer a clatty, wee bitch," and slap me. I would be crying, and the more I cried the more she slapped me. "I'll give you something to cry about," she'd shout. Now after this, she'd put paraffin all over my head, which burned my scalp terribly, and say, "Where's the money they gave you?" I would reach into my pocket and pull out a £5.00 note. She'd say, "Is that all they gave you? You're not hiding any back for yourself are you?" I wasn't. Sometimes I did though. She'd take the money then send me to my room, as my head was stinking of paraffin and sore. I would go into the wee back room, as we called it, and tell my dolls, Jenny and Mary, and my imaginary friend Mary Hopkins what had happened, and then fall asleep.

Afterwards, I'd get shouted at for my tea, well we called it our tea, it was evening dinner, as my dad would be in from work, and he always asked, "Where's the wain?" Then my old mo would pretend to be all nice to me and Dad knew nothing. After tea, I would go to bed, though sometimes I got a bath. Water was scarce, so the bathwater was used for all the boys and the rest of the water was left for me. I came out of that bath dirtier than I went in. I never felt clean as a child, I was so dirty with tidemarks round my neck and ears. I was never washed by my old mo, I was always expected to wash myself, and the soap stank. It was soap my dad would bring in from his work called carbolic. My body and hair I would wash, with this soap, in the filthy bathwater that was left for me. The neglect as a child I had was horrific.

I also remember when I reached 11 years old, I ran away. I asked my wee pal Roslyn to come with me, so she did. We hitch-hiked down to Wemyss Bay which is about 6 miles from Greenock. We were out very late. Roslyn's mother had contacted the police and all the neighbours in her area, which was also Stafford Road – the top end, I lived at the bottom – all of them were looking for her. No one was looking for me. The police found us two in the train station in Wemyss Bay. They took Roslyn home first. I remember her mother crying, she was worried sick but so glad Roslyn and I were all right. Then the police took me home. They knocked on my front door, and my old mo answered it.

The police said, "We found your daughter, Mrs. Harrison."

My mo said, "How? Where was she?" No one even knew I was missing. I felt so jealous of Roslyn, as she'd had everyone looking for her, and no one in my family even knew I was gone. We were gone for hours. This was 12 o'clock at night when I was taken home.

I will never forget the look on the policewoman's face when my old mo said, "Didn't even know she was missing." Then I got a slap, was told to go to my room, and how dare I bring the police to the door.

The police were always at the door, as the older brothers drank a lot of alcohol – it was very much an alcoholic household – then they'd fight like mad with knives, slashing each other, and the police were always being called. I would hide under my bed terrified, listening to all this.

I was riddled with fear at a very early age. I used to pray to God, well a crucifix with Jesus on it, and ask him to help me not grow up like them, as the noise and screams of my old mo were terrifying. I knew I wouldn't get abused these nights though 'cause they'd be in jail overnight, so I used to thank my crucifix for peace and an undisturbed night's sleep. I always prayed before I went to sleep, and I always blessed everyone in my family, even my old mo who I prayed for even though she was so cruel to me.

As we were very poor, I didn't have the toys and stuff my wee pals had. At that time, all young girls saved up scraps, which we called mottoes, they were like angels and glossy, coloured pictures you put into a collection book and swapped with your friends' scraps.

I didn't have any, so my brothers Joseph and Vincent cut pictures out of a catalogue and told me, "There, you have mottoes now that you can swap with your wee pals."

Well one girl, Anne G, had the best scraps ever, big, fancy angels and cherubs. I swapped all my catalogue cuttings with her for exchange of her good mottoes, but when she went home and showed her mother, her mother came charging down to mine, raging and telling her all about what I had done. So I got slapped again and made to give Anne G back all her good scraps, though I would skip a page so I at least had some nice mottoes. The catalogue cuttings were clothes, furniture, shoes, etc. just cut out the catalogue. It was funny when I think back on this, only my brothers could think of such crazy ideas. It was so I didn't feel left out with other kids, but it just made it worse, so no one would swap scraps with me ever again. Funny at the time, I may add.

I also remember, I was around five or six years old, my friends had lovely, pink plastic beads and earrings. I was so jealous, I really wished I had beads and earrings too, so I went in and told Joseph, Vincent and Edward.

They said, "Don't worry, hen, we will get you beads and earrings," and so they did. It was macaroni, dried and painted, with a piece of chewing gum attached on each, so they could stick to my ears, and a melon seed necklace all painted different colours. I was so happy. I went out to play the following day with my new jewellery on to show it off, when I got bullied and laughed at because they were handmade, it also didn't help the fact that it was macaroni earrings and a melon seed necklace.

I always felt out of place with some of these girls, 'cause they all had a lot more than I did and they would laugh at me. I would go home crying. That night John comforted me, then abused me, and told me his pal owned a toy shop in Lynedoch Street in the town, and that I could go up there any time and get beads, rings, earrings and mottoes or scraps. So one Saturday morning, I jumped on a bus, still only five or six – no one asked any questions, as my dad was a bus driver and all the drivers knew I was Wee Johnny's daughter, so they'd let me on without paying. I remember, just as if it was yesterday, getting off the bus and going into, as I was told by John, the second blue shop in Lynedoch Street to see a man behind the counter.

I said to him, "My brother, John Harrison, sent me up. He said you would give me mottoes, beads and a necklace."

He walked round the front of the counter, went over and locked the shop door, put the closed sign up and pulled me towards him, saying, "You're Wee Sandra then."

I said, "Aye, at's me," meaning yes, that's me, then he pulled out his penis and told me to touch it and I could get anything I wanted from the shop, so I did. Then he told me to pick some things I wanted, so I took scraps, beads, earrings and rings, well one ring. I said thanks, and he said I would have to come back tomorrow and I could get more, so I did knowing I would have to play with his cock but then get the pick of the shop.

I did this for weeks, until John got a hold of me and told me I had had enough, not to go back to the shop and to say that he bought me the items if anyone asked. So I did what I was told, only to get abused that night again by John. He knew the shop owner, so John was in control of me not going back.

He said, "Fuck him. He's had enough of you. Do not go back." So I didn't. I'm not justifying the shop owner at all, but I was only told to play with his cock and show him my vagina.

I told John this, but he already knew what I did. As I stated earlier, John knew everything that was happening to me, and so he told me it was now time for one of the regular predators to take naked pictures of me. I loved the camera. I did think the pics would have only been of my face, but this predator took Polaroid pictures of me naked, opening my tiny, wee legs to let him take photos of my bum, front and back, and for this I got paid £5.00 or £10.00.

I never told my old mo about the photos, but I reckon she knew 'cause John would have told her. She and John had a weird relationship, not like mother and son, more like mother and boyfriend. She used to tell me to call him my dad, and I refused bluntly to do this, as I knew he wasn't, then she'd batter me stupid and send me to my room. People would ask where I got all the bruises, and I used to say I fell all the time. My father was always out working, so he didn't have a clue what was going on in the house.

I called 4 Stafford Road the House of Horrors, and then, when I was 11, we moved over to 3 Stafford Road, as my father had a really bad accident at his work. He was driving big cranes to move stuff from one place in the Scott Lithgow shipyards to another, when the crane went out of control. My father was in his cabin, 50 feet up, and the crane was holding very heavy materials, which was just about to crush his cabin. People stood below in horror. My father had to jump for his life. He was in hospital for six months, and they thought he would never walk again, but he was a very brave, wee man. I remember coming in from primary school to hear my old mo, and other people, talking about how bad my father was, though no one told me. I ran into my room, knelt down and cried to the black crucifix to help my dad and make him live. I couldn't imagine my life without my wee dad. I loved when he came in from work, usually at all different times. My old mo didn't, all she was interested in was his pay package. Well my wee dad came home in a wheelchair.

He said to me, "Don't you worry, hen, I will walk again."

I used to birl him round in his wheelchair, and we'd laugh like mad. My old mo hated me and my father laughing.

She would shout, "Will you shut it. Yer gaen me a sore heid." This was telling us to be quiet. We were giving her a headache.

My wee dad, my father, I called him my wee

feather, he would say to me, "Sandra, please don't grow up and be like her, hen," as my old mo was a very heavy gambler, she was at bingo every day and night, and was also a very bitter pagan Catholic.

She used to shout, when Celtic and Rangers football teams were playing, "Come on Celtic, beat these orange bastards." She said that 'cause, at that time, my father walked with the Orange Order band, and he was going back to his Christian faith which was Plymouth Brethren. My old mo hated them. She said they were evil people.

At an early age, my father used to read me stories from the Bible. I loved this, but my old mo would go crazy. She was as bad as the nuns that taught me. She'd say that the Bible was for priests only, so my feather would wait till she went out and tell me the stories. When I could read, he gave me my first ever Bible which I had to hide from my mo. She'd go mental if she knew I had a Bible. Even though she used to make us go to church every Sunday, it was Roman Catholic Church. My brothers would hide in the forest, where the chapel was, and send me in to see what colour the vestments were, which was the colour of the robe the priest was wearing, 'cause my old mo would ask us, when we came home, to make sure we were there.

At this time, my mo was trying so hard to move across the street to 3 Stafford Road, as it was flat, with not so many stairs, and the back and front doors would be easier for my dad to get in and out. She also wanted to move away from the big family that stayed upstairs, one being one of my predators. So when she found out that the lady who lived there was moving, she asked the council right away and she got it.

My father was getting slowly back on his feet. He started going back up to Kilmacolm and the Gryffe, helping the farmers with the tomato plantation. He would wake me up at 5 a.m. in the morning and take me with him. I loved it. I would go into the cottage, called Garshangan, and Jenny and Willie Kerr would greet me with the biggest smiles and a welcome I loved. I would help Jenny prepare the workers' 10 a.m. cuppa. She'd ring a bell to let them know tea and jam sandwiches were ready. Everything was organic; the milk, she made her own jam and bread, they grew all their own fruit and veg and sold them to every shop in Port Glasgow, Greenock and Gourock. Their products were amazing. Their daughter Mary took a shine to me, and she treated me very kindly. I got so close to Mary.

I remember one day, up the Gryffe, tents were being put up in another field, and I asked my dad, who was in the big greenhouses picking tomatoes, "Can I go over?"

He said, "Yes, on you go, hen. You'll meet some nice people over there." So off I went. I was made so welcome. There were loads of kids from all over having so much fun, swimming in the burn, as we called it, and then sitting telling Bible stories. Sometimes we would go on a picnic.

I do remember a girl saying to me, "Have you been saved?"

My answer was, "No, I'm a good swimmer. I have never needed to be saved." She just laughed and told me that's not what she meant, so I asked one of the leaders that were there, or the teachers, and one lovely woman explained that it was taking Jesus into your heart to save you. I was so young and didn't realize what this really meant. I was to ask Mary when I went back to the cottage, and she explained it to me. As I was brought up very strict Catholic, I thought Jesus was still on the cross, so how did I get him off the cross and into my heart? Mary told me to pray for this, not to a crucifix, just to Jesus himself who had risen from the dead. She told me Jesus was no longer on the cross and that it was not good to pray to a crucifix or statues, as in the Bible it said do not worship graven images and that's what they were. I reckon that was the day Sandra received God into her heart, as I felt great. I told my dad on the way home from the farm.

He said, "That's good, hen. You better no tell yer mo, she will stop me taking you up to the Gryffe. She thinks these people are the devil's worshippers." How wrong was she, so I said nothing.

The tents were only there during school holidays, June to July, any other holidays they were not there. They called it Bible camp. This didn't stop me going up to Gryffe with my dad, as I felt so safe and so wanted by these lovely people. The only thing I couldn't understand was if Jesus loved me that much how could he let this horrific abuse happened to me? Now I'm older,

I realize it wasn't Jesus, it was the devil working through people. I suppose that's why they called paedophiles beasts, as in the beast himself.

I hated leaving the farm at the end of the day, as I knew my father would go out to his local pub the Greenock Juniors, or sometimes the Larkfield No. 2 Club, my old mo would go to bingo and, as usual, I would suffer abuse at the hands of these beasts. I prayed God would let me, or help me, stay up the Gryffe, or stay with my wee Granny Beanie in Duff Street, in Greenock's town centre, but this was not to be.

Then, just before we moved to 3 Stafford Road, my nephew and his father came home from Australia for a year; Frank, the dad, my sister Ruby's man, and Wee Johnny. I so loved Wee Johnny. I took him everywhere with me, and I tried my best to keep him safe and away from the paedophile ring. Later on in life, I found out they got hold of Wee Johnny too. I was so upset, as I thought I'd protected him. I was only 10 to 11 years old, but I did feel like he was my wee brother. Wee Johnny was only five years old and a very bad asthmatic. Somehow the Scottish weather helped his asthma stay stable. I didn't realize, but while Frank and Wee Johnny were in Scotland my sister, Frank's wife, went away with another man. Frank was devastated. This was a sister I never remembered, I didn't know her. My father disowned her from the family, as he was dead set against divorce.

After a while, I was just starting secondary school, we got the house across the street. While we were all busy moving furniture across the street, one of my predators, Tom, let me in what we called the spare sitting room, which was only for guests, in 4 Stafford Road. He put furniture against the door and proceeded to rape me. While he was doing this, I was lying with tears streaming down my face, wishing he would hurry up, and also listening to people move furniture across the road to 3 Stafford Road. I remember my old mo saying leave the big guest room till last, as this had all the good furniture in it and a phone as well. That's why he had taken me into this room. I do remember the phone ringing which startled him. I jumped up and ran out of the room. I was so scared, as I went across to our new house.

I was told my room was the front room, facing the street, and it had a red plastic door on it. I asked my brother Edward to put a lock on the inside of my door for me, so he did. That was my safety lock. I was never abused at night again in that room. Not that John, Billy or the other predators wouldn't try to get in, 'cause they did, so still my sleep was getting disturbed with them attempting to get it in my room, but they could never get in, and I would pretend to be asleep and not hear them. Both of these houses were infested with mice, though, and the noise of them scraping, inside the walls, terrified me so sleep was always hard.

I would go to school with no money for the bus, so I had to walk over the reservoir, which took me 20 minutes to get to school, only to go to class and fall asleep. I always ended up in the medical room, where I would sleep for hours, until I was woken up to go home, when I had to walk back the way I'd come.

I had lots of friends in school, new ones I'd met, especially Karen.

She was getting bullied from the other girls, and I stuck up for her, saying, "You hit her, or shout at her again, you'll have to deal with me."

I had a bit of a reputation at this time and

wasn't scared of anyone, so Karen became my closest friend, even up to today she is. She called me her protector and, needless to say, Karen never got bullied again.

When I was 12, I used to play truant from school, we called it 'skigging' school, and I was sent a social worker. When he came into the family home, my older brother made friends with him and made a point of putting him off any scent of my abuse; that's how cunning, baffling and powerful this paedophile ring was.

I also wasn't very clever in school, though it did make it worse that I was dyslexic and it was never picked up. Although Karen and I were very close, I never told her about my abuse – I never told anyone – and the abuse was still going on. Now the paedophile ring was 23 adults. I just accepted this and that it was my fault all along. These 22 men and one woman, who was a lesbian, groomed and sexually abused me in the most horrific way and programmed my brain to their sick, sick way of making me believe this was why I was born and they all owned me. I was threatened with torture, death and beatings to keep my mouth shut, called every filthy name under the sun and tossed aside, like a piece of unwanted rubbish, when they'd all had their sick way with me.

I remember being tied to a bed in 3 Stafford Road and sexually abused. Again everything was done to me, and I was made to do things with my mouth to them, except vaginal penetration. I would even throw up at times and, being tied up, I nearly choked on my sick.

This was John or Billy playing games with me, saying, "Let's tie you up and tickle you to death." They made it sound fun and a good game. I'd let them tie me up, and it wasn't till they sexually abused me that I would learn the hard way not to fall into that trap again. All my predators made out it was only a game, and it was a secret game, no one was to know as it was between us. It wouldn't really matter anyway, because if my own mother and a parish priest didn't believe me, what chance did I have?

I wished my life away, always saying, "When I'm 16, I'm out of here," and I meant it. This time, in 3 Stafford Road, the alcoholic house once again, the same as 4 Stafford Road, it was still as bad with fighting and trouble. The police were never away from the door. Billy would batter his wife then, Sandra, to a pulp every time he was drunk, and everyone in the house would fight. One minute we were all singing, my three brothers on the drums, guitar and keyboards, me singing, everyone dancing having fun, even my old mo would join in, until someone said the wrong thing then all hell let loose and usually blood was everywhere. I'd end up hiding upstairs in my locked room, with my wee niece Mary terrified, trying to keep her calm, until the police came and then all was silent. Usually Billy and John got lifted, and their friends that were drinking with them too. They all knew John was weird, that was a major reason for them to batter him. The thing was, John got battered and stabbed for something that they were doing themselves, but I couldn't say anything through sheer fear. I knew they were all guilty of abuse, sexually and physically, and that John was the scapegoat for them all.

Somehow, in my heart, I knew someday I would tell my story. It took years, as I was trying to deal with a normal life through abnormal circumstances. My head was so screwed up, I thought my abuse was love and I was special to them all, that's why they chose me. Well, it didn't help when I was constantly told I was their special girl, better than anyone. I got this attention and liked being everyone's special girl, I just didn't like what they did to me sexually and then the beatings, especially by my brothers, if I refused. I always had black eyes, broken arms and was bruised terribly with the torture I received. John only battered me twice, but Harry and Billy beat me up terribly. When I was a very young child I remember Harry's beatings, and then at 10 or 11, Billy's beatings, they were the worst. I had to go onstage with sunglasses on in the winter to hide my two black eyes. People thought this was just part of my costume, the sunglasses, but everyone else in my family knew I was getting beaten up except my dad. The other brothers couldn't stop this, as they were getting beaten up too. Although I had six brothers, the three older ones were the predators. My other three brothers got the same beatings until they grew up and rebelled against them, especially Joseph. I always said he was my saviour, as he beat the shit out of the older three every time he found out that they'd battered me but, as my close three brothers grew up, they hated the older ones, and I knew for a fact if they'd known the extent of my abuse, along with my dad, they would have killed the older ones and that's a big reason why I never told. I didn't want them to end up in jail, so I kept quiet.

Moving over to 3 Stafford Road was mayhem. Everyone was carrying some sort of furniture, or clothes, across the street with all hands on deck. I couldn't wait to get into my new room, especially with the lock on it. Once we'd moved in, we were without carpets for weeks. I had a single bed, a built-in, cupboard-like, small wardrobe and an old dressing table with a mirror on it. I always looked at myself in mirrors – I still do it today, it's a safety thing – as I always thought I was an ugly, smelly, wee tart, as I was often called, and had to look in the mirror to see. It was Mary Kerr from the Gryffe who told me I was beautiful and God's child, and I had to look for the beauty in me through the mirror. That became a daily occurrence for me.

I remember taking all my posters of my pop idols down from my wall in 4 Stafford Road and thinking I could put them up in my new room and also, as I walked out of 4 Stafford Road, I was so happy, as this was a house of horrors for me, and I thought 3 Stafford Road would be a safer and different for me. Well I was wrong on that one, as I would still be in the hands of the predators. Even though they couldn't get into my room, they got hold of me at any chance they could in other rooms, or even in the garage that came along with the house. The thing that hurt me very much was that my old Granny Beanie wouldn't see my new house, as she died just before we moved. When me and Wee Johnny, my Australian nephew, went to see her in hospital one Saturday afternoon, as my old mo couldn't go due to her bingo addiction, when we got to the hospital the nurse took us into the back room, then my Aunty Ruby, my mother's sister, came in, she was also my godmother, and told me and Johnny we would have to go home, as my granny was dead. I cried my eyes out, took Wee Johnny's hand and walked home. He was so young, he didn't understand. I was only 11, so it was also hard for me to take in that I would never see my granny again. That was the first time I had experienced a death of someone so close, and it hurt so much.

If that hurt wasn't bad, I also had to come to terms with my first wee boyfriend's death. His name was Dennis. I was very fond of Dennis. He was in my primary class. Every Friday, in the last year of primary school, St. Andrew's Catholic School, we got taken to Hector McNeil's swimming baths, the whole class. I loved this. Dennis and I were always together swimming. Then one session, Dennis stopped in the middle of the pool and just sank to the bottom. I tried to pull him up, but couldn't. I started screaming, then two lifeguards jumped in, cleared the pool, and one got me out and the other got Dennis out. I didn't need to be resuscitated, but Dennis did and was brought back to life lying next to me. They took Dennis away on a stretcher.

I remember him saying, "I'm OK Sandra," and smiled. I waved at him, and then was taken into the medical room of the swimming baths and given the all-clear to be taken home by the teacher. Then at teatime, my teacher appeared at my house, in 4 Stafford Road, to tell me Dennis had died in hospital. I was gutted. This was not long after my granny had died. Then the Daily Record was at my door and wanted to interview me and to ask me all the details about what had happened. I remember my dad being there, and I told them what had happened. They then asked me if I had a picture of Dennis, which I did in my school bag. I gave it to them then cried, sobbing my heart out. My dad told the two reporters to leave, as it was too upsetting for me. I went to my room and cuddled up inside my bedcovers. I was told later that the police were also in the house, but my dad would not let me speak to them, as I had fallen asleep.

Dad said, "I think my daughter has been through enough for one day."

I still remember trying to save Dennis and couldn't. I blamed myself for years after this for his death. I also developed a fear of water and never swam for years and years after it. On that Monday, the whole school was in mourning. It was sad. Even my teacher at that time was in tears in the classroom. These two deaths had happened just before we moved across the road, so I always said 4 Stafford Road was cursed. I hated that house.

Although still young when we moved into 3 Stafford Road, my abuse was still going on. It just became acceptable to me, it must be me, it was what I wore, or how I spoke. I blamed myself for what my predators were doing to me, especially John and Billy, as Harry went out to Australia to join my three sisters. I found out later he was abusing my three nieces in Australia. Then it came to the time for Wee Johnny to go back home to Australia, along with his father, Frank, who was a really nice man. He hated John, and every time they drank together they would fight like hell. I was later to find out that John had been abusing Wee Johnny also. I cried when Wee Johnny left – he was named after my father.

I used to play with a girl in the same street. Her father was abusing me every time I went into her house, so I stopped going around with her. My brother John knew this, as they were, as I called it, in the ring together. I was asked why I didn't go to the house any more or go in the car with him and the other men. I said I didn't want to any more. I lied and said I'd fallen out with my friend, his daughter, but John would say I'd let him down. I was to try and find some other younger girl to take my place, but I couldn't and this was one of the reasons why I'd run away.

At this time, I was still carol-singing, had a paper round, went to the shops for neighbours and began to babysit, along with taking kids out for walks in their prams. I would also get paid for this. Again, this money would be taken off me by my old mo. I got wise to this and also wanted to buy myself clothes, as my old mo made everything I wore. I wanted clothes the same as the girls in my school, so every week I would go into town, or down to Gourock, and buy myself clothes, telling my mo one of my friends had given them to me. I began to make more money for clothes. My old mo would buy me the odd pair of shoes, but I had to start getting shoes too. Being dressed as a tramp for years in primary school, and getting bullied because I was dirty with second-hand clothes on or something my old mo would knit me or make me, I loved getting my own clothes.

I started to become very independent at the age of 12 or 13. I used to even buy my own dinner at night, 'cause I was sick of the cheap meals my old mo was putting giving me. I used to throw my dinner down the toilet pan, pretending that I'd eaten it, and then go to the chip shop for a portion of chips and sweets or biscuits. I babysat a lot, and when I was off school on holidays, my dad would still take me up the Gryffe farms to help with the tomato plants. My dad would occasionally go up to a house in Langbank to work in their garden. The lady there had three daughters, and she would ask if I could babysit for her, so I did. At the age of 13 she took me to Arran with her family. I watched the kids, helped them with their homework from school, and she would pay me a good wage. I loved this job as it made me money and got me away from the alcoholic house that 3 Stafford Road had turned into, plus I was away from my predators, some of who had now moved on to other children, saying I was too old now I was 12 or 13.

At this time, I remember one night all my friends and some family members were sitting on the steps outside 3 Stafford Road, when one of my predators came up to me and told me to go into my room, which was upstairs, as they had something for me. I thought I was getting a gift or something, but no. I was to have my light bulb taken out of the ceiling, and with my room in darkness, I was pushed down on to my bed to be abused by two boys older than me.

My brother's voice was in the background saying, "Hurry up! You no finished wi' her yet?" I was crying and told to shut up, or I would get something to cry about. I don't know who these boys were to this day, but I do know my brother set it up. Just as he would bang on my bedroom door at night, telling me to open my door, come downstairs and entertain his drunken friends. He didn't mean just singing, which I still loved doing. He would want his drunken friends to drool all over me and kiss me, so I would always pretend to be asleep. My old mo would say she never heard a thing, yet she slept in the next room to me and she didn't drink alcohol, but my dad would have been out cold drunk, so I know he didn't hear him shouting and banging on my door.

"Come on, Sandra. I'll pay you for it," he'd say. I still never answered, only then to be called a selfish, little bitch.

Although we had moved to 3 Stafford Road, just across the street, the house was still full of drunks and paedophiles. The one that killed my tortoise was always hanging around, and at times he would play with his dog's penis, making me watch this, and if I didn't he'd set his dog on me. It bit me a few times, on the back of my leg.

I also got a new kitten from the pet shop, which I tried my best to hide from my older brother, but when he entered the house one night and saw I had a new cat, he said, "Yes, no long before that one sufferers too."

I would beg him, "Please don't hurt my cat," but as it got older it was terrified of him. I couldn't understand this, because he said he never hurt the cat, who I called Kitty, until one night I came in after playing at a friend's house, and he kicked my wee Kitty cat so hard she flew up in the air, came down with a bang and was crying terribly. I was screaming and jumped at him, trying to kick and punch him, but he ended up beating me up terribly. My two older brothers came in, dragged him out of the house and kicked him all about the garden. Just before they got hold of him, I smashed a milk bottle and stuck it in his arm; it was him or me, as he was beating me up so badly I was going down. Then my two brothers took him out. I phoned the police, and he got lifted. I had to hide from this older brother, Billy, for weeks, as he was going to kill me.

I also had a rabbit called Tufty, and he fed my pet rabbit to a dog we had called Fang, a German shepherd. He was a sick, sick, sadistic human being. His sexual abuse stopped when I was 15, but that was because I kept saying no and running away, but my physical abuse got a hundred times worse. It was the same with John, and my other predators said I was too old now anyway, I was 15, and they needed younger meat, as they called me, so I became so rejected, unwanted and beaten to a pulp any time they got hold of me. I hated myself so much.

In fact, at the age of 14, I tried to cut my wrists, well I did cut my wrists, as I wanted to show them, especially my old mo, exactly how I felt. She just battered me, along with one of my brothers, while the blood spurted out of my arms. She then took me to hospital, to lie and tell the doctors I fell. The doctor wasn't daft. After he'd stitched me up, all 27 stitches in my wrists, he mentioned a psychiatrist, but my old mo refused and got me out of that hospital so fast. She didn't want anyone like that talking to me, as they'd get to know too much, so this wasn't to happen. She then proceeded to tell my dad I fell too. Why she lied, I don't know to this day. I was dying to tell the doctor I did it myself, but she kept shaking her head at me, so I just agreed with everything she said. When we got home she put me in my room and told me I was in there for good, never to come out of the room again, as I disgusted her, so I took to my room for days, with no food or water. I'd sneak down to the kitchen at night, when they were all asleep, and make myself some food and a cup of tea. I was also off school for weeks. I used to go to bed at night and wish I would never wake up. I hated my life, I felt so trapped in that family, it was horrendous.

It seems so unreal, this story of mine.

I didn't go to bingo often, but one night I did, and four women came up to me and said, "You're wee Sandra Harrison, aren't you?" The bingo is full of noisy, gossiping women, so I was hoping no one would speak to me, as I didn't mind. Over the years, when I sang in the Mecca bingo hall, firstly with the San-Karen Band, which included me, Karen, my great pal from school, my brother and three other guys, we had a Mecca contract. I was only 17 when I sang with the band, and the Mecca bingo was just in Greenock at this time. It had been Vincent who had encouraged me to get on stage and sing professionally. He's taught himself to play the guitar since he was 11, and he's always been really good. I think it was his coping mechanism and me getting on stage, singing, really helped me with my confidence.

There were two other bingo halls, but Mecca was the biggest and best payer for their entertainment. I loved this, this band were amazing. We had a great name all over Scotland, and we were all very young then. My other pal, Tricia, was to join us, making it three girls and four boys. We were so popular all over. We played in the 20-minute interval that the bingo had when no one played anything, and it was always a full house.

As I sat in the Mecca recently, there's not as many people nowadays, and in the interval everyone plays mini bingo or the machines, the slots, so entertainment doesn't happen very often nowadays.

So here's me, and the first woman to talk to

me says, "Ah, you look so much like your wee dad. What a lovely wee man he was," as Dad would sometimes go to the bingo. This woman didn't mention my old mo, but I do remember my mo talking about her.

"That Bella," she'd say, "Nosey bitch. Tell her nothing," she'd say to my dad.

Then another woman stopped me in the toilet. "You're Sadie and Johnny's daughter, wee Sandra Harrison."

"Yes I am," I answered, trying to make a quick exit.

"Your mum was a lovely woman. Everyone in here loved her. She was so funny."

"That would be my old mo," I said.

"It's funny though, she would always talk about her boys [my brothers] but never really mentioned you, Sandra. Did you go to Australia too then with your sisters?"

"No," I said, "there was just that many of us, my mo couldn't keep up with who was who." This was my exit line.

"Nice to speak to you, hen."

"You too," I answered, and then out I went only to sit beside this wee, frail, old woman called Lily. I remembered her coming into my mo's house; she smoked and liked a wee drink. She also lived across the street from my brother Billy, the bully. She didn't have a good word to say about him.

I said, "I don't speak to him at all. He's a very nasty man."

She agreed, then she mentioned the thing that most people wanted to say to me and that was, "I saw your brother John in the papers during week. He got eight years for abusing seven young children, boys and girls. Is this true?" she asked.

I said, "Yes, and it's about bloody time he was locked up, that beast."

Well she looked at me with 'oh my God' eyes, as if she knew I was one of those children.

She said, "I was always worried, years ago, when he owned garages, as my son Jim worked for him, and there was a lot of talk then about him hanging round kids all the time."

To put her mind at rest, I said, "Don't worry, Lily, Jim was not abused by him, and he's behind bars now, so they'll slap it into him." I just said that about Jim to calm her but, in all honesty, I am pretty sure he got hold of Jim too, as being a serial paedophile, I don't think any young person escaped the abuse from John.

"Anyway," I said, "let's not talk about it, Lily."

And she said, "Your mother knew about him, she just turned a blind eye."

At that moment I felt sick. Holding back the tears, I was glad when they started calling bingo numbers again. I never spoke again to wee Lily, as she was off talking to someone else. I was glad.

Just as I was walking out of the door, Izzy shouted at me. I hadn't seen Izzy for years, so I went over to speak to her.

She said, "You must be gutted about John and what the paper says about him."

Well it was front-page news and said: 'Greenock man gets eight years in prison for preying on seven young boys and girls in Greenock, the youngest being only four years old. That child told her mum what was happening when she was six, only to get a slap and called a liar.'

Well then the tears came running down my face.

I said, "Izzy, that four-year-old was me."

Well, she just grabbed me tight and cuddled me. "I'm so sorry, Sandra. This must be torture for you."

At that point I broke down again, and I didn't feel like I could control my emotions and my flashbacks around all the trauma I'd experienced, but Izzy seemed to want to know more and wouldn't let me get away.

I didn't know what to do, and in a blind panic, I managed to get rush out of the Mecca to where I'd parked our van. I drove off in a whirlwind of tears and emotions, wanting to escape from it all. I just felt like I couldn't deal with any of it any more, and I decided I would leave Greenock and run away, so I just kept on driving.

As I started to drive out of town, I began to calm down and realised that I should not do anything stupid or it would jeopardize my case, and also, the case being so big, it wasn't worth it. So I stopped the van, and I said a prayer to God to help me find the strength to not show my hurt to my husband. God was on my side, as I pulled up on my drive with the van the rain was beating down, not unusual for Greenock, so by the time I got it in the front door I was soaking wet, and went straight to the bathroom to get dried. I just got in a bath, as I always do when I think about my abuse, as I still feel dirty and a bath seems to cleanse me and calm me, so my husband wasn't any the wiser. I didn't mention anything but didn't ever want to go back to the Mecca. In fact, I struggled to go out at all, as I felt 'Abused Child' was printed in bold on my forehead, and also, being very popular in the community, at 57 years old, everyone knew me or I knew them and that happening to me, being so confident on stage, singing and acting and entertaining still, people just couldn't believe the life I'd had, as the secret had been kept for all these years.

Looking back now, when I was 13, I started my periods.

I was terrified to tell my old mo, 'cause she always said, "When you take your periods that's when you sin against God." But my cousin was staying overnight with me, wee Katy, and she couldn't keep her mouth shut. She stayed with me a lot. I reckon she was never abused in my house, because she was so mouthy and told everybody everything. Well Katy told my old mo.

I will never forget her running upstairs. "Tell

me if you kiss any boys now. You know you'll get pregnant and shame the whole family." I felt awful and wished I hadn't started them.

It was a Saturday and, come Monday, I was sent home from school, as I'd fainted and had bad cramp. My teacher dropped me off at home. My dad was in, and I told him what had happened and asked him not to tell my mo, as it would only be an inconvenience for her. So Dad made me up a bed on the couch, went to the shop and got me some sanitary towels, as I had none. My old mo never bought me them, deodorant or shampoo.

She would say, "Just cut up sheets. That's what I had to do when I was young."

That horrified me, so Dad bought me some Dr. White's, told me to always wash down below and that the instructions were on the back about how to use them. He also gave me a couple of painkillers. This was to happen to me every 21 days, so any money I got, whether it was for getting abused or working after school and at weekends, all went on toiletries and sanitary towels for myself, which I had to hide in my room so none of the boys would see them. I also had to wash all my own sheets and underwear, as my old mo would have gone mental at me if she'd seen any bloodstains.

As I was always fainting, I decided to make an appointment myself for my doctor to check me over. Well, the doctor diagnosed me as being anaemic, short of blood, so had to put me on iron tablets, and I was on them from 13 until I had to have an emergency hysterectomy when I was 33. I didn't mind, as it practically saved my life, and I already, at that age, was married to my first husband with a boy and a girl and with no plan for any other kids. Thank God, as that marriage was a flop, ending in divorce.

So there I am, 13, on iron tablets and starting to look forward to my periods coming, as I knew this was a great excuse for me to tell my predators I couldn't let them touch me as I was bleeding. From 13 to 15, my abuse got less and less. This suited me fine. I was not being abused sexually as much, but I was getting physically abused, battered, when I said no.

One time, one of my predators, I will call him Tom, grabbed me in the garage at 3 Stafford Road, ripped my blouse apart, pulled my bra up and was licking my breasts, dragging my long hair that it hurt. I told him I was on my periods, so he slapped me across the face so hard that my ear was stinging. He pulled my hair with one hand and squeezed my boob that hard it was sore. I was so afraid, I wet myself. It was running down my leg and some urine went on his shoe. He called me a clatty, wee bitch, slapped me again and pushed me over, leaving me lying in a heap in the dirty, old garage at the side of our house at 3 Stafford Road. I managed to get myself up and into the house, where I stripped naked and got into a cold bath, as there was no hot water. I scrubbed myself, as I felt so dirty. I cried and cuddled up at the end of the bath in the fetal position, feeling so cold and numb. I eventually got out, covered myself with an old towel that lay on the floor, picked up my clothes and ran upstairs and into my room with the lock. I managed to get clean clothes on and put the clothes I'd been wearing in a plastic bag. My hair was still wet, and I didn't have a hairdryer, so my hair would have to dry itself. I took my bag of clothes and threw them in the bin.

This predator, Tom, was related by marriage

to the family. He was partying and drinking alcohol, dancing and playing cards with my brothers that night as if nothing happened; another sick beast. I was only 13½ years old, and he was in his mid twenties. This was the same man who had put the furniture against the door in 4 Stafford Road. I know now he had raped me. It took me years to say that word, rape, as I couldn't accept I was raped, not by just one of these beasts, but 22 or 23. They weren't all forceful with me, most of them would make out it was a game, or that I was their girlfriend or special wee sister. There were a few times, when I started drinking at 14 years old, I would wake up in the morning with my pants down to my ankles, my back bum bleeding and just know I had been abused.

I started drinking a lot and drank to get drunk and black out, because then I wouldn't know what was happening. Also, I could cope when I was drunk, as it blocked my abuse out. I started to fight back when I was drunk, only to come out the worse. My brothers Billy and Harry were the worst for physically beating me up, so when I got drunk I used to challenge them to fight me.

As usual, I always lost.

My life now was so downhill, I stopped going to the farms with my dad and became a rebel. I was still singing in the family band, as I loved entertaining, I felt so wanted with a crowd. I got the attention I wasn't getting at home or in reality. My schooling suffered badly. They transferred me to college at 15 to finish off my last year in school. I chose to do window dressing. I loved it and met a whole new bunch of friends.

When I turned 16, I left college with no job, but I was very happy, as my sisters and nieces were all coming home from Australia for a visit. When they arrived, my dad hired a minibus for them all. This was the first time that I'd met my Australian family, as I couldn't remember them that well when they went away. I wasn't very nice to my sister Kathy, as I thought she'd just abandon me as a child, so I would speak to her, and I wasn't shy in telling her I didn't like her. My sisters knew nothing of my abuse, and no way was I going to tell them.

I got very close to my niece Linda who was the same age as me, and I vaguely remembered Linda as a child in Scotland before they all left.

Linda and I were 16, and Linda introduced me to whisky and Coke. We used to drink it together in my room. We started to share a lot with each other, and I was to open up and tell Linda of my abuse. Linda was to tell me my other brother, Harry, was abusing her in Australia, and she couldn't get any peace away from him. Linda and I told each other everything but swore to keep it a secret, 'cause we were so ashamed and both thought it was our fault. Linda and I stuck together, while my family stayed for three months.

At this time, the San-Karen Band was at its highest peak, and I had my first real boyfriend, who I loved dearly. I will call him Eric. Eric was to take my virginity, though I did ask him to. We went out for a few years then split up, which broke my heart. I swore I would never let a guy hurt me ever again as bad as that, and I kept my word, I never did.

With my family back in Aussie and Eric and I finishing, I left home and moved over to Dunoon to get a job in the Tornade Hotel as barmaid, cleaner and kitchen maid. I didn't get paid, but I got my own flat in the hotel and got very friendly with Wilma the owner's daughter. We used to have a live bands on at the weekend and discos on Wednesdays and Thursdays. Mostly our guests were Americans who worked on the ship the USA Holland. They would stay for six months at a time, and I had to get up every morning at 5.00 a.m. to cook breakfast for them. There were around 10 of them, and there were other people who were holidaymakers. I loved that job, and it was great to get away from the family in Greenock. No one missed me, of course, except my wee dad who always asked after me. All I did in the Tornade was work, sleep and drink alcohol.

I was then introduced to an American called the Doc. He was a lovely man and became a good friend. We used to smoke pot together. This was the only time I smoked it and felt good. I couldn't smoke it with anyone else, I would feel too paranoid. I never smoked it a lot, so when the Doc left to go back to the USA, I never smoked it again, I always preferred to drink.

Before I knew it, I was slowly becoming an alcoholic. I drank every day. I would get totally wasted, and Wilma would have to carry me to bed. I wasn't singing at this time, but I did write a lot of songs which disappeared somewhere along my drunken life journey. Drink had become my crutch. I could deal with life on life's terms with alcohol. I just loved it, playing the clown all the time at parties in the hotel. I still never went out with any other boy, as Eric was still in my heart.

Then one day, a massive blow came. The owner, Wilma's dad, said the hotel was going into liquidation and would have to close. Well, within three weeks, the Tornade closed its doors. We were all devastated. Wilma and I stayed with her sister for a couple of weeks, then her dad and his girlfriend got a rented bungalow in Partick, so the four of us moved up to Glasgow Partick. I lasted only eight weeks then came back to Greenock.

This is when I met my first husband and couldn't wait to get married, to get out of the madhouse of 3 Stafford Road. So I did as I said earlier, I moved to the village of Inverkip, I gave birth to son and daughter, drinking alcohol, got a hundred times worse, moved back to Greenock and right back into my old mo's house. She was quite happy, as she was getting good keep money from us.

I was so scared, in that house, to let my children out of my sight. Thank God, we moved again, through the council, to a housing scheme called Branchton, which was wild, staying in the village for eight years. It was a complete culture shock for my children to move to Branchton. They had to change speaking really properly to 'common as muck' to fit in with the other kids, although they still travelled up and down to Inverkip School. That marriage came to an end after another two flats which were private lets. Then I got lucky. I got a three-bedroomed, back and front door, up the Bow Road in Greenock, Graham Street, a brand-new house with lovely neighbours and only six houses in this small street. I couldn't wait to move in. I arrived with no carpets, curtains, cooker, fridge, suite, anything, just me and the kids plus clothes.

My ex's sister also moved in with her son, as she'd sold her house and was waiting for a new one. She was there at least eight months, which gave my ex an excuse to move there too. I ended up leaving, to stay with my brother. When my brother asked me whose house Graham Street was, I said mine.

He said, "Why are you sleeping on my couch with the kids if that's your house?"

So he took me over and helped me throw my ex and his sister out of my house. That is when I got my freedom. I felt great. It was just me and the kids, and a wee Lhasa apso called Bud. The kids were now in their secondary school, the Greenock Academy, and I was just totally wasted with alcohol. I wanted to stop drinking and have a better life, but I just couldn't. My house was like a local pub, drinking and partying, with lots of people coming and going. I was so drunk, at times I didn't know where my kids were.

I would invite all sorts of people into my house, as long as they had drink, even my brothers who'd abused me. I sat and drank with them, listening to a load of shit about why they'd abused me, trying to justify it by saying it was to teach me about life, and it happened in all families, and that we should just put it behind us because it would destroy me and I'd end up in a mental institution. I believed this crap, and they were happy to bring alcoholic carry-outs into my house for parties. The drink had such a hold on me I couldn't say no.

There was still a lot of violence in my family. I started going over to my old mo's, drinking with the boys, and then fighting with them. With my mouth dressed, I could give my old mo her character too. I became wild and didn't care who I hurt. You see, I wanted revenge but was doing it all the wrong ways, under the influence of booze, now I had become a raging alcoholic.

Everyone I knew drank alcoholically. If you didn't drink, I didn't want to know you. I used to sit in pubs and clubs and drink with anyone.

If there was anyone beside us that didn't drink, I would say, "Watch them. They don't drink, so don't trust them. Watch what you say in front of them."

Also, I would steal people who were sitting with me's drink if they went to toilet. They would have been so drunk too, they didn't notice. I used everyone I could to get my fix of alcohol. I also became a pest; no one wanted me in their company or house, as they couldn't get rid of me.

One of my close friends had a bar in her house, she was also a singer. By this time I'd stopped singing, as I wasn't fit enough to go on stage, and was hanging around with drug addicts and alcoholics. Drugs were never really my scene, although my predators had topped me up a few times with amphetamines so they could do what they wanted, but I put a stop to taking that as drink was best for me, it blocked everything out, all my fears and past memories.

So back to my friend with a bar in her house. She made the big mistake of inviting me back to her house for a drink – big mistake. I was still there two weeks later. She had to ask me to leave. The only way I would go was if she gave me money and one of her nice bottles of wine, of which she had many. Before I took the wine from her, I checked the alcohol's volume. Well, she'd given me one with seven per cent alcohol in it.

I said to her, "You're joking aren't you? I wouldn't even put this on my chips, as vinegar has more alcohol than this." I was so angry with her, although she wasn't to know about volumes. I was the raving alcoholic not her. So just to get rid of me, she let me pick my own bottle. Well I was in my glory, getting the highest volume wine, and I had the cheek to ask her for a couple of cans of lager, because if I didn't drink them, I said to her, I would go into a seizure and die, which was bullshit, I never had a seizure at any time, but she agreed. I left her house was £20.00, plus two bottles of strong wine and two cans of lager.

She lived in Dumbarton, so I had to get a train to Glasgow Central and then one to Greenock West, which I did. I thought I had just won the lottery – I had a drink and money – so off I went on the train to Glasgow. While I was on the train, I opened a lager; that was a curer, as I called it. I didn't have a train ticket, but the train was so busy, I hid in the toilet until the train ticket collector went past. Soon I had finished my lager and was in Glasgow Central. I went down to the toilets in the station to drink my other can. Now I was feeling the drink hitting me. Again, I ducked the train fare. I just sat in the toilet on the train for the whole 45 minutes and drank a bottle of the wine I had, then we reached Greenock. I ran upstairs on to West Station feeling so proud. I had dodged paying two train fares, and I still had £20.00 and a bottle left. By this time, I was staggering about.

I stumbled into a bar, close to the station, and the girl at the bar said, "Sorry, I can't serve you,

you're too drunk."

I started giving her dog's abuse, shouting at her, "I will be back to wreck your pub."

I began to walk home, as no way was I paying for a taxi or a bus. I didn't live far from West Station and just had to walk through the cemetery. When I got into the cemetery I decided to sit at some random grave and open the other bottle of wine which had a cork in it. I searched about for something to stab the life out this cork, to get the bottle open, calling my friend of all the bad words I could think of, saying she'd meant me to pick a stupid corked wine I couldn't open. It didn't occur to me that in five minutes I would have been home and could use a corkscrew. I was so desperate, although so drunk, to get this bottle open and into my system. I found a bookie's pen, a very small pen you get free from bookies, and I started to work on the cork. With a lot of picking and anger, I eventually got the cork pushed into the bottle, put the bottle to my mouth and slugged away.

Lots of people used the cemetery as a shortcut, so when people passed me, I just got that look of disgust from them. In my sick head

I was thinking, They're just jealous they can't do what I'm doing, drinking outside during the day and not caring a jot. At some point, I crawled up to some secluded bushes and fell asleep.

I woke up some hours later. It was dark and the cemetery was locked. I had to climb the wall and stagger home. I just fell in through the door, crawled upstairs and pulled the covers over my head. I woke up hours later, the next morning, to be violently sick. I couldn't stop being sick, and I knew the only cure for this sickness was another drink. Then I remembered I still had £20.00.

I asked my neighbour, "Please can you go to shops and get me a couple of cans of lager for my hangover."

To which he said, "First I have some vodka left from last night. Would you want that too?"

I jumped at the chance of that offer. He poured me a very large vodka and Coke and set off to the shops for me. I was shaking so bad, I couldn't get the glass to my mouth. I got a straw from the kitchen cupboard, left the glass on the table and sucked through the straw. I retched a couple of times. I started praying to God, who I didn't believe existed, to help me keep the alcohol down. After a few attempts, it stayed down and I stop shaking, and then the door went with my delivery of two cans of strong Pils lager. I was happy, as I knew I would get through the night.

At this time of my life, my family had all left. The kids were teenagers and out doing their own thing, and I was on my own feeling the loneliest person on the planet. Once I got the bravado to go out, I knew one of my drinking buddies had a gun in his house. He was all legal and had a licence for it, so I went up to his house and asked him for a loan of it.

He took me inside and said, "What do you want a gun for, Sandra?"

I told him I wanted to shoot the people that had harmed me when I was a child.

I told him some of my story of abuse, and he said, "OK, let's teach you how to shoot." So he showed me how to load the rifle, placed a target on his wall and told me to practise. So I did, and I began to like the sound of the gun firing.

He then said, "We have to go out and practise on wildlife first." So we went back into the cemetery to look for anything that moved.

A police car was driving round the cemetery,

and he threw the gun away and rolled me and him down a hill, and we hid until they went away. Still with alcohol fresh in my system, I couldn't care less, but my friend was terrified. This made me think that it was all lies, and that he didn't legally own the gun. With luck on our side, the police never caught us, and we left the cemetery.

He said, "Leave the gun. I will hide it and pick it up in the morning." I just went home, and he went up to his own house.

That night was the first time I experienced night tremors or the DTs some call it. I was alone in house, with my wee dog, terrified, shaking so badly I started seeing things that weren't there. It was hell, and the devil was staring at me from the bottom of my bed. I grabbed the old crucifix I'd had as a child and held it so close to my heart. Screaming and crying out for help, I cried myself to sleep.

I woke up the following morning with a feeling that I didn't want to drink again. I was too sick, and it was going to kill me. I knew drink was my coping mechanism, and I could block out all my past. You see, I had blackouts, which meant you would wake up after a bad binge and wouldn't remember where you were or what you'd done.

I lay in bed, sipping cold water, thinking that was the end of my life; that it was over. I was contemplating suicide – not just cutting my wrists – I was planning to take all of the pills I had in the house. For some reason, I thought, Before I go, I'm going to confront my predators and tell them I'm committing suicide because I can't deal with my traumatic childhood and my excessive drinking. So I telephoned my brother.

He said, "Come down. We will speak about this. You need help, Sandra," he said, "and I'm the only one that can help you."

This was during the first ever time that the tall ships had visited Greenock.

So I went down to his house, and I asked again, "Why did you do this to me, yer wee sister?"

He said, once again, that it was to teach me about the sexuality of life, and that if he was doing it no one else would have come near me.

I said, "They still did. They all knew you were doing these things to me, and you knew they were doing it to me too. Don't lie to me any more. I need answers before I die."

He tried to cuddle me, but I froze; that beastly look still in his eyes.

Just then his partner came in and said, "What's up? Why are you here, Sandra?"

Just as I was going to tell her everything, my brother put a line of amphetamines in front of me and said, "Go on, you'll feel better after this." So I took it. I was weak and so vulnerable. Then they both took it, and the next thing there was a double Bacardi and Coke was next to me.

Every time his partner left the room, he also said, "Sandra, you ask me to show you these sexual things when you were a child. I wouldn't have touched you if you'd never asked. I also gave you everything you wanted. You didn't suffer."

In my mind he was right, so then I blamed myself. It was all my fault. It must have been, to have 23 predators who I knew, and others I didn't know. Yes, he'd convinced me. I'd asked for it at a very early age.

I cried and cried. I felt so guilty and dirty. He held me and said, "It's OK. We all do things in life we regret. We just have to forget it ever happened."

That was me, 34 years old and back to that

child of six blaming myself. His partner came into lounge again.

I wiped my tears away and said, "I'm sorry. I'm just very depressed."

She poured me another drink. "This will cheer you up," she said.

Then after a few drinks, I was pissed again, and they both said, "Would you like to come over and meet Eddie and Avril?"

I said, "OK."

They stayed in a cottage on the beach, but when we drove into their drive something stopped me going in. I simply refused. I felt something wasn't right. Then my brother said OK, 'cause I'd started to get angry.

He said, "I will just ask Eddie for the motor for the boat, and we can go up to see the tall ships."

I sat in the car, and he went into Eddie Kerny's house. I didn't see anyone, just a shadow of someone opening the door. My brother came out with the motor for the boat and off we drove, just about 200 yards, to the sea where my brother's small boat was. It looked more like a raft than a boat, but we went back to their house, which was on a big, private estate in Wemyss Bay, and packed bags of booze, sandwiches and snacks. We left and went down to the boat. It was very small, could only really just hold the three of us, and there were no life jackets, and off we went towards Greenock to see the tall ships, drinking as much Bacardi and Coke as we could. I was absolutely mangled.

I can't remember anything after going to see the tall ships. I just remember waking up in my brother's house, in bed with his partner. Nothing happened, it was just sleeping. Then in the morning, I asked them for money, a loan, and they gave me £65.00 and dropped me off at my home in Graham Street. My son and daughter were in and asked if we could go down to the tall ships. I said yes, so we did, bumping into their dad. I ended up drunk again and inviting him back to the house. After drinking and getting drunk with my ex, the alcoholism ripping the insides out of me again, that's when I left and went over to my other brothers. As I said earlier, my other brother took me home and got my ex and his sister out of my house, and I never saw him again.

I was back on my own in Graham Street. I had money, so I decided to just throw the towel in and get wrecked again. I went and bought a bottle of vodka, sat and drank on my own with all my childhood pictures scattered about the floor, feeling so alone, ashamed of myself, hating myself. My self-esteem was so low, I really did want to die. I started drinking vodka straight, and the last thing I remember was crying into my childhood pictures.

At this time, my old mo was still alive and so was my dad. I couldn't phone them, my dad wouldn't speak to me when I was drunk, and everyone had blocked my number from their phone, as I was a pest, and they didn't want to still be talking two hours later.

I woke up on a grave in the cemetery, and I didn't know how I'd got there. I was clutching an empty bottle of vodka, praying to God to put some in it for me, and if he did I would only drink half pints of lager. Making deals with God, pleading for his help, I looked at my watch. It was four in the morning. I managed to get on my feet and crawl home, my head spinning. I got to my front door that was still open, and only my wee dog Bud was in. The place was a mess. I even had my electricity meter rigged, as I paid no bills at all. There was no food in the house either.

I poured a glass of water, walked to the toilet, stumbled across a Yellow Pages, and opened it up to see Alcoholics Anonymous staring me in the face. I really needed help and maybe this was my help, so I picked up the phone and called. On the other end of phone was a man.

He said, "My name is Donald. Can I help you?"

Well I broke down and told him, "I need help. I can't stop drinking."

He was so nice on the phone and said, "Have you any drink in the house?"

I said, "No."

He said, "That's good. When was your last drink?"

I said, "About six hours ago."

He said, "Don't lift another drink, and someone will be with you soon," so I tried to tidy up a bit, and then the door went.

Two AA members, a male and a female, came in and spoke to me. I actually thought they were going to tell me how to drink properly and maybe have a wee curer for me, but that was not the case. They told me they were alcoholics and that they hadn't drunk for several years. I was astonished. I didn't think it possible to not drink alcohol for that long. They started telling me their story and how AA helped them never to drink.

They said, "Do you want to go to a meeting?"

I said, "No, not today," as I was shaking.

So they said, "Don't lift that one first drink, and you won't crave another until tomorrow, as it's only a day at a time," and they left their phone numbers for me to call if I felt like a drink, and they would come and pick me up in the morning to take me to a meeting.

Morning came and, true to their word, they both came to collect me and took me to an AA meeting. I was terrified, shaking, and people kept giving me tea and making sure I was OK. They were very nice people, telling me there was life after drink, I would be able to cope, I would have a life beyond my wildness dreams, and that I was no longer alone, although I felt like the loneliest person on the planet.

These people were all around me, giving me

hugs and saying, "Keep coming to the meetings, Sandra, we are here to help you."

I was so distrustful of people, I just wondered when the final punch would come. Like, now you have to do this for us, or pay, or something. I was sure they wanted some sort of payback from me. This AA fellowship was just too good to be true. One thing I knew, I didn't want to drink alcohol again, so I decided I'd stay for the time being, then I could run out when things got dodgy.

Then they mentioned God, and I thought, That's it, a cult, a religious cult. So I mentioned this to a long-time sober gentleman, and he laughed.

He said, "You find a higher power in here to help you keep sober, and some people choose to call him God." Well drink had such a powerful hold over me that I didn't think anything could get higher than alcohol.

I was told, "Get a sponsor [this is a close-mouthed, trusted friend who would keep you right] and keep coming to the meetings. You will change into a better person than what you were when you were a drunk."

So I thought, What the heck? What can I lose?

I had nothing to give anyway. I was spiritually dead, up to my eyeballs in debt and had no friends, as they were all still in the pub. So I picked a female and a male sponsor, and they both got to work on me. I was put on a programme of recovery, a 12-step programme, a programme of freedom and which was life-changing. I attended meetings every day and night. I went out of town with my sponsors accompanying me. I was lucky to still have my wee car but never had any petrol in it, so anyone who came with me in my car had to buy it for me.

It came to around six weeks, and I felt that over those six weeks the alcohol was coming out of every pore in my body. I started to feel good, and I learned I had a serious illness, alcoholism. I had to accept I could never drink again or it would be death, jail or insanity for me. I realized, after being a few months sober, as I used to count the hours I was sober, the days and the weeks, now I was into three months of sobriety. Never since I was the age of 13 had I ever been three months sober, I'd never even been three weeks sober, as I didn't know any sober life or sober people. I was feeling great and every day I was getting better.

My sponsor told me, "Now, Sandra, it's time to change your old self and become a good, sober mother, friend and person."

"How do I change?"

"Start by liking yourself."

As I said before, when I looked in the mirror I hated what I saw, so I started taking care of myself, cleaned my act up and was also told everything had to be sobriety, there was to be no alcohol at all. Weddings, parties, Christmas, this all stopped.

I started to stand up in meetings and say, "My name is Sandra, and I'm an alcoholic" and really mean and accept this. I could not lift that first drink.

I started to look back at my life, but then my sponsor told me, "Don't look to tomorrow and yesterdays gone," but I couldn't get the shame, remorse and guilt from my head. My brain was racing. I was told to, "Keep coming to the meetings. This too shall pass." These are all sayings in AA meetings.

Now I had started to have a completely different crowd of people as friends, who loved me unconditionally. I couldn't believe it, I was on my journey of recovery. My ego was massive and my self-esteem was zero. I didn't think, at times, I could do it, to not to drink again. Then I started sharing with different people and, to my delight, they all had felt the same as me, I was getting identification.

I was asked to go to an AA dance, so I went along. Well, that's when I found out I couldn't dance sober. I was so paranoid.

I said to my friend Grace, "While I'm dancing all these folk are staring at me."

She said, "No, Sandra, you're not that important."

This made me furious and have some resentment towards Grace. I had to learn that I'd brought this all on myself, so that was first time that I did.

I started a journey of growing up in AA. I went into the rooms with a 14-year-old head on me and I was actually 47 years old. I did what I was told, got into AA and all its works, and I became Sandra again, the one that came into this life, the clean, sober woman who could face her fears and deal with life. I started to like myself, but my past, historical abuse kept pushing me down, and my nightmares started to get worse. You see, my mind had opened up, and it started to know the truth about what had really happened to me. Sandra Harrison, an innocent child, came into this world and was used and abused from the age of two to at least 16, although I still had my virginity. I lost that after I was 16, but I had lost everything else.

My nightmares were always about my predators trying to catch me, and I would keep running and running. I would actually go into a dream and relive this childhood trauma and wake up curled in a wee ball at the bottom of my bed, terrified. My nightmares are still with me at 57. I just have to try my best to deal with them, as living through past trauma of cruelty, neglect and sexual abuse is horrendous. Although, I do believe you have to run the gauntlet to get clear to the other side, and the more you do that the more it reveals itself. It's like all the poison these beasts put into me as an innocent, little child is all cleansing me inside.

As I do feel spiritually clean, I only have to deal with nightmares without popping sleeping pills. I'd prefer not to take any mind-altering drugs at all. I do feel it's the devil's work. Maybe that's why paedophiles are called beasts. The devil was a beast, it says that in the Bible if you're a believer. I sit tonight, just after another horrendous nightmare, where I woke up terrified. Once I'd calmed myself down with water and two paracetamol, as my headache was so, so bad, I had to sit and reprogramme my brain and keep saying "Sandra it's just a dream. It's not happening," then after a good two or three hours, I was ready to accept that it was just a dream now, but that scar will live with me forever.

I sit, at times, and try to imagine what went through the sick paedophiles' brains when they were abusing me. I mean, a child is so innocent. I just can't get it out of my head how much of a neglected childhood I had; no mother to protect her only wee baby girl. Being a mother now myself, I totally believe my children. I would believe a child before I'd believe an adult. The scar of childhood sexual abuse will always be with me till the day I die, I just have to make sure it doesn't get me to distrust my faith, as I think God was holding me in his arms and could not stop the paedophiles from hurting me. They said in the Bible there is a judgement day, when we all die, so that's when the people who hurt me, and also so many other kids, will suffer and have to account for all the evil things they did.

I feel so sick when I see my niece right in amongst crack cocaine and alcohol. I have tried to detox her so many times. I lost my other niece to drugs also, but it's so sad when I think that on her death certificate it said a drugs-related death, when I think it should say another child abuse case with drugs blocking the horrific memories of it out of her mind, that's why my nieces took drugs and alcohol, and drugs or alcohol are to blame for their deaths. It completely breaks my heart. I understand people using these things to block it out, but drugs and alcohol kill you. It's only the truth that can really set you free.

Thank God, I have the strength and faith not to have these addictions, or mental health issues, which happen to mostly girls and boys who have been sexually abused as children. Some of my friends are dead now from taking their own lives, as they couldn't cope with the shame, remorse and guilt of getting sexually abused as kids. Is this normal human behaviour? If so, this to me is hell on earth.

One of my friends was sectioned recently because of self-harm, but it made me so angry that no one, neither doctors nor psychiatrist, had asked her, "Did you get abused as a child?"

The answer would have been yes, as I knew. I seem to know if people have been abused, it's as if I have an insight to their minds, but I think it's because I was, and I can spot the triggers and the way girls and boys, men and women, act, speak and behave. I also seem to attract victims. I really get exhausted with trying to help, as I see me in them and know the hurt so well. Although I have yet to meet or speak to someone who has been through as much trauma as I have. I think of the grooming process they all used, years before they actually abused me. They got me to trust them, feel as if I was the most special girl in the world, and this they did until I refused and said no at the age of 15. I said no, and I stayed out of their way as much as I could. This didn't stop them from looking and finding me, filling me up with drink and drugs, and saying I asked for it. I have found out that paedophiles do not change at all, once a beast, always a beast. I do fear for my niece, as she was abused by the same people that abuse me.

I had to speak up to the police and CID about what happened to me. It took a lot, and the trigger for me was a murder, a murder of a special needs girl who was tortured and abused sexually. I read in the papers about this poor girl who was murdered. The so-called carers, also one of my brothers, John, were supposed to be looking after a girl called Margaret Fleming. They tortured and killed Margaret, and set her up with a boy to try and have a baby for them, as my brother John and his partner were so desperate to have a baby they would go to any lengths. His partner, being a midwife, would have possibly been there to deliver Margaret's baby, although this was a conversation I overheard in my old mo's house, there was never any solid proof. Police Scotland and all the authorities dealing with this case never found Margaret's body. My brother and his partner, at this time, were also trying to buy children. My niece was pregnant, and they offered to buy her unborn child. They also were so desperate to have a child that they would ask any vulnerable, pregnant lady to sell them their baby.

Once they were going through IVF treatment. I found out the name of the private clinic they were using in Glasgow, and I phoned, letting them know they would be giving a child to two predators and, if they were not stopped, I'd go to the press with this information. Luckily the clinic did not agree to their terms, and they struck the two of them off from using or receiving IVF. I was so proud of myself when I made that phone call, as I knew I would be saving a child's life from torture and abuse. My brother said he would kill the person who'd made this allegation and call. I believed he would have no idea who to trust any more. This was my total faith which kept me honest.

I sit here in the villa, across from the Panorama building in Torrevieja, Spain, with my feet so, so scarred by the burning, hot ashes that I was put into in the bin when I was two years old. My feet still flare up with the effects the burns had on me. As I look down at my feet now, I can't imagine why that man, Alex Robertson, could torture such a child. I trigger terribly and have to pray my feet cool down, and also remind myself that I'm not that two-year-old child, it's not happening now, I'm 57, but it sure feels like it. I dare say this is past trauma. These monsters, who damaged and scared me, will be judged, and they will burn in the fires of hell. I only get these angry thoughts when my feet are bad, as I know the damage must have been so horrendous for a child. I'm glad my memory of this event is blank. I cannot remember being in that bin with roasting, hot ashes from my old mo's fire, but my feet keep reminding me, especially now they have flared up again, and I have to ask my husband to give me a pair of cotton socks to cover up the burn cream I have to use, the socks covering the cream which cools the soles of my feet.

I also, as I clean the apartment, remember that Cinderella feeling, of being a child in a big family, especially the youngest, before me six boys.

I cleaned, cooked and tried my very best to please my mo, so I would get, "Ah, look what our Sandra did. You're a good lassie, you know."

I'd feel good, as I had been praised for the work I did, although my hands were sore, sometimes my knees with kneeling down on a hard surface to scrub the floors, only for them to be filthy with oil and petrol half an hour later from the brothers that were mechanics. Well, Edward was the only qualified mechanic. John was self-taught and stole Edward's papers and certificates – which he'd studied hard to get, he even went down to Oxford for his full-time mechanic degree – but because he was J. Harrison and John was J. Harrison, this was identity theft on John's part. Edward did all legal work, and John took all the glory. Sometimes, at night, I would come into the house, and it was more like a scrapyard than a home with dirty, oily engines lying all over tables and the boys trying to fix the parts. I didn't mind, but just after I had scrubbed the oil, petrol and grease from the table and floor, I knew I would have to do this all over again just to get praise from my old mo.

The cooking wasn't so bad, we would take turns me, my old mo and my dad. Only when my dad cooked, wow, the dishes I had to wash then were a bit much. You see, my dad was a cook on the boats at sea and cooks had galley boys to do all washing up. Well, I felt like a galley girl when my dad cooked, but I loved his food, the end result was always beautiful to eat and well-cooked. The only time I hated dinner time was if there was tripe on, which is one of a cow's stomachs. Rubber would have been easier to eat, so I would do without. Thank God for free school meals, I'd say. Sometimes I'd get pig's feet to eat, they were called pigs' trotters, and I couldn't eat them

My old mo would say, "Well, you'll get nothing else if you don't eat what's put down to you." I'd just starve rather than eat pig's feet or tripe.

My old mo's macaroni was good, so when that was on the stove I'd be so happy, as I knew I would get a good, hot dinner with home-made chips. My father used to make wedding cakes. I loved it when he did, as he would give me the spoon to lick after he'd put icing or buttercream on it. This was such a treat for me that icing. My dad made it so good that you could roll it out and just place it over the cake. Also at Christmas, Dad always made Christmas cake which was usually a small, cottage-type house and everything on it you could eat. He'd mould a wee girl out, put her in the garden playing, waiting for Santa Claus.

He'd say, "That's you, Sandra," and I'd love this.

I also helped him with mixing the food colouring. The wee Christmas house always had a thatched, brown roof, the house was always white, a lovely green garden with snowflakes and me with a wee ball. He would make it as if I was building a snowman. My dad was very talented and artistic with his cakes, and they were in demand by half of Greenock. I loved that time of year, Christmas. I am pretty sure I believed in Santa till I was 14 or 15. I think I just didn't want the build-up to Christmas to ever end. I'd sit and wait for the Beatles' film to come on TV, I just worshipped Paul McCartney and John Lennon, they were my favourites, and they would show all of their films, always in black and white. It took years for us to get a colour TV and when we did, out came my most favourite film The Wizard of Oz. Oh, how I wanted to be Dorothy so much and fly over that rainbow. I would sing along with this film all the time, I loved it, I loved singing. Then I would impersonate the wee munchkins and the wicked witch. I had great ways to make everyone laugh at Christmas, me pretending to be all these characters.

"An actress," my dad would say, "our Sandra, a bloody good actress and singer."

I loved the attention I got from this and also making people laugh. It was great, until the alcohol came into the house with my older brothers, and the more they drank the more all that anger, frustration and madness would start. The fighting was horrendous and then the police were called. Billy was the worse for being a bully and hurting my cat. He tortured it, starved it so badly, I had to get the vet to put wee Cheety Face, I called him, to sleep. This was heartbreaking for me, although funny for Billy. He was very, very cruel to my animals. So Christmas came in merry and went out very sad. My old mo would blame January. She used to say January was an unlucky month for everyone, so January every year was very negative for me. It was as if they gave you the good gifts and smiles then tore them straight out of your heart. I always cried in my room on Christmas night, lying listening to the carnage alcohol had brought into my home again, praying to make it all stop. The police would arrive, so you could say my prayers were answered, and some of the boys would get lifted, kept in jail overnight. I used to wish they would keep them in longer, especially my three older brothers, the beasts I called them.

I do remember buying all my family Christmas presents with my carol-singing money. It wasn't much, but I would buy my dad a small tin tube of petrol for his lighter and a packet of cigarettes papers. I'd also buy my other brothers who smoked this as well, which were three oldest, then I'd buy my other three brothers sweets, like a box of Smarties, a bar of chocolate, or even a Mars bar. They all would thank me. I also would get my old mo bubble bath or some nice-smelling stuff she could use. I never missed buying my brothers presents, even if it wasn't much. I loved to see them opening it up, thanking me and making me feel so good. I loved giving. I was always a giving person and loved the look on their faces when I did.

I do remember waking up one Christmas night to the smell of paint. I thought Santa was painting in the living room – we called this the kitchen and the kitchen was called the scullery.

As I sneaked into the kitchen, to my surprise there was no Santa, only my dad painting a desk and chair for me that he had just made and a doll's house. I didn't want him to see me, so I sneaked back to bed and never mentioned a thing, only to get too excited about getting up in the morning to play with my doll's house, and my desk and chair, to my surprise, had my name on it, Sandra. I was so happy with these the next morning. My doll's house even had lights in it – a bulb wired up to a battery – and little stairs, little windows that opened and little doors, plus the roof came up to let me open the house and that way I could play. It had little handmade furniture too. The only thing it didn't have was any people in it so, with my plasticine type of putty, I made my own little people, as I couldn't get my baby dolls in the house as they were just too big.

One year, I got a big spacehopper and bounced up to the shops with it. Only, to my sadness, it burst as I bounced on glass. This was the bottle of milk I had been carrying, so the family could have a cup of tea, so I cried again, threw my spacehopper away and lied to my old mo that it blew away, or she would have belted me badly for bursting it. I found out, at an early age, that if I cried first, I wouldn't get beaten up or slapped so hard by my old mo, so I was now called a greeting face, wee bitch most of the time. I always got embarrassed when I cried, so I would show my old mo my tears then run and hide somewhere. I can still do it today. That wee child within me pops up, and I have to remind myself that I'm not that wee child now, no one is going to slap me, and it's OK to cry, as it is a human emotion. Sometimes I would cry that much as a child, I felt I was actually drowning in my tears. An overactor they'd say, but they'd not have a clue about how sore my heart was, or still could be if I lived in the past, which I refuse to do as it's not healthy at all for me, but you see I trigger a lot, especially when I go away with my husband on holidays. If I go out of the country of Scotland, I think I should not be there, that I am not good enough to visit beautiful, hot countries, especially Spain, when I should know the Spanish language, as my father's mother was fully Spanish, hence that is where my sallow skin comes from. I am embarrassed to say I can't speak Spanish, that's one for my bucket list.

I sit here now in my camper van, which is called Bert, a Mazda Bongo my husband bought for a bargain, and we are in Millport, on a little island across from Largs, which is 20 miles from Greenock. I remember as a child being taken to Ardentinny, and it was the highlight of my holidays.

"Keep the wains aff the street," my old mo would say, and I felt so safe there. Nothing happened to me in Ardentinny, as long as my predators were not there. Oh, but this was not to be. Again they'd know where I was and come over. Yes, over they came knowing me, little Sandra would be there. My dad would be in the Ardentinny Hotel or drunk in the tent. We had tents first, and then we moved up the ladder to a very small caravan which used to be an old fish van stinking of fish. I will never forget that smell from a two-berth caravan.

It was an old lady who owned the farm we stayed on. Me and my three brothers, who I loved dearly, used to go there with my old mo to visit her, as she was kind enough to let us camp in her fields every year. She was a lovely old woman. We would go into the farm cottage, and she would come out with a plate of biscuits. We would sit there, me, Joseph, Vincent and Edward, look over at my old mo, she would nod her head to signify yes, and we would take one biscuit each. If the old lady passed the plate around a second time, we would look at our old mo, and she shook her head to signify no, so in turn we would all say no thanks. We daren't take a second biscuit 'cause we would have got slapped and called greedy wee baskets.

The old lady had a horse in her field, and its name was Smokey. I loved this horse so much and so did my three brothers. We used to pick grass and feed it. One day, a bus of tourists stopped and gave us bags of sweets and cakes to feed the horse but, as we were starving, we decided to eat them ourselves, lovely hard-boiled fruits and bits of apple pie, I fair enjoyed it. Poor Smokey, she just got more grass, while me and my three brothers munched away. Funny now, when I think of it now, the old lady also kept bees and used to make the most beautiful honey I'd ever had, even better than my granny's, Old Beanie, who bought hers from the first supermarket I ever knew called Liptons. I would add some of this honey to my porridge in the morning.

"You're bloody English," my old mo would say, "it's salt you should use," so I would put some in when she wasn't looking. I loved the sweet taste of honey in my porridge. Sometimes it would be jam; that was even better, as I knew, as a treat, we would get bread and jam later on before bedtime. We called it a 'chit in jam' or a 'piece on jam'. The farm, on the other side of where we camped, would make strawberry jam and give it to us. They grew the most delicious strawberries I'd ever tasted. I always remember the farmer, he was so nice. He would tell me how I had the most beautiful eyes he'd ever seen. He was lovely. I knew right away he wasn't a paedophile, and I could trust him. He would bring the strawberries and walk me round their farm which was huge.

I loved Ardentinny. The only bad experience was when an predator of mine, from Greenock, came over. In our street, when I was young, everyone knew everybody's whereabouts. So this time, we had a tent and the old caravan that used to be a fish van, and it was all family and friends camping in Ardentinny, loving it, running wild in the beautiful, green fields. The country roads had very few cars and there was an amazing beach, half with sand and the other half rocks. We had fires on the beach at night, hot tea made on the fire, with a piece of bread and jam alongside, amazing, and I also met a few friends that lived in the village. They were so nice. I couldn't believe there were no bullies there. They were all such lovely people on this little farm and in the village. Then comes over, from Greenock, the predator, pretending to come and join the family and friends on holiday. With eyes constantly on me, I felt so uncomfortable.

He would always slap my bum and say, "There's my special, little girl." These words still makes my skin crawl.

All the young kids would stay in the tent, and the adults would be in the caravan drinking alcohol, or over at the hotel. That day, my predator came over. He had plenty of money, so he was welcomed with open arms, as that was alcohol, cigarettes and food for everyone.

He whispered in my ear, "I have money put aside just for you, my special girl. I will give you it later if you're a good girl." Everyone thought he did this because I was the youngest and the only girl, well that's what they'd say anyway, but my three older brothers would know what the money was for if they saw me with it.

Well I knew what he meant, so I kept as far away from this man as I could. But one day, me and my new village friend, Barbara, were playing in her farm's barn, and he came in.

"So here's where you girls are hiding." My heart sank.

I said, "We are just going down," as you had to walk downstairs from the top of the barn to get outside to the farm. Just then Babs, as I called her, her mum called for her, so she left. I was alone with this monster.

He came right up to me said, "I told you, wherever you go, Sandra, I will find you. You're my girl remember." Then he pushed me down in the hay, lifted my skirt up and abused me.

I was just a sweet, innocent child aged, at this time, eight or nine, one minute laughing and playing with Babs, throwing hay everywhere, to then be lying under an old drunk who was kissing me and touching me inappropriately. I would just have to lie. I could feel my tears running down my face. I was so scared, I couldn't move and felt numb lying there, looking at the sky through a window, a tiny, wee window in the roof of the barn, wishing that this abuse would stop, praying for help, and then hearing footsteps below.

He stopped, jumped up from lying on top of me and quickly threw a £5.00 note on my lap, then said, "See you later on then, my little Sandra," and patted my face. He knew I was crying, as his hand could feel my wet tears. "What you crying for? Only big babies cry. Stop crying or I'll take that money back," then he left. The footsteps were Babs coming back to play.

I remember telling her I fell, that's why the man stayed with me a while, and that's why I was crying. Lying again I was. After playing, Babs's mum, also known as Barbara, shouted us in for our tea which was delicious, steak pie, mashed potatoes and turnip, and a large glass of milk, a real treat for me that was. She said my old mo sent that man over to the farm to make sure I was OK, but I knew this wasn't true, as she couldn't care less about where I was.

I knew the old pervert would have said, "I will go check on Sandra. Make sure she's OK."

Also, this was one of the predators I had told my old mo about and what he was doing to me, only to be called a wee liar, a storyteller, a gub. This really hurt me.

After a lovely tea at Babs's, we walked back to our campsite, which was not far from the farm. Babs's mum walked me over, as it was dark then, and there were no lights in the village, you needed a torch to get around, and the midges would eat you alive. It was good Babs's mum smoked, as this helped keep them away. The bats circled around us, but these things never scared me, I only ever had a lot of fear when my predators would get hold of me. So I did have good times, I just shut all the bad out and pretended it never happened.

On the way back, I could hear them all singing around the campfire and, as I got closer, I saw my predator along with my other three predators all sitting with my old mo and the rest of my family and some family friends. There must have been around 20 people there, mostly adults.

I went into a panic, I was so, so scared, and I asked Babs to ask her mum if I could stay overnight at her farm, as I knew my predators would get hold of me that night if I stayed there.

So Babs begged her mum, "Can Sandra stay overnight?" And her mum said yes. I was so, so happy, I skipped all the way over to the fire to tell my old mo I was staying over at Babs's. I didn't have to ask her, as she couldn't care less where I stayed.

So Babs's mum said, "Is it OK for Sandra to stay over with Barbara tonight Sadie?"

The answer was, "Aye, course she can," but the look of disappointment on my predators' faces was a picture. I smiled and walked back to the farm. I stayed with Babs that night, and it was to become a regular occurrence. My predators had no chance of getting me now, so I would just love my Ardentinny holidays now. Twice a year we went and I always stayed with Babs. I felt so safe in that farm. I used to wish Babs's mum could let me stay there forever and, you know what, my old mo would not care a jot.

She would say, "At least I'll get peace from that yin. She's worse than all my boys put together." Then my dad would pipe up and protect me from her verbal insults. They would argue. My old mo would say, "Daddy's lassie, eh?" She hated the attention I gave my dad and the love he gave me. She would threaten not to take me back to Ardentinny, as I was getting too spoiled over there, but of course my dad put his foot down on that one.

"Sandra doesn't come, neither am I," he'd say. My old mo wasn't happy about that. I just loved that small village. Ardentinny wasn't far from Dunoon. In Ardentinny, my dad taught me how to find shellfish. These things we found were like big muscles, they called them clabby doos, and also a little, round, snail-like shellfish which were called whelks. You boiled these in hot water and the clabby doo shell would open up to reveal an orange-like shellfish delicacy. Now if you were lucky, you would find a real pearl or two inside the shell. I was always lucky, I found pearls all the time.

I loved this, as my dad would say, "For every pearl you find, Sandra, make a wish."

As I loved singing, I always wished to be a famous singer with my own records being played and dreamt of being on TV singing. I always wanted to be loved by everyone and also be a big star. I know now I sought and loved the attention, and that I put down to not getting enough attention as a child.

As night fell on Ardentinny, we would all sit by the beach fire and sing or tell stories. I loved this. There were good times in my childhood, I made my own fun. I used to love going out and picking brambles and blackberries. Dad used to make the best jam ever. I also would pick plants and flowers and press them in a book, and Dad taught me how to make coloured paint from wild flowers or wild berries. I used to paint pictures with the bright yellow dye from wild flowers or purple from blackberries, even red from a red tree berry. This was all so magical to me. I also picked crab apples. Dad said they made the best apple pie. He taught me how to make jam, apple pies and even sponge cakes. My old mo never spent time teaching me anything, all my knowledge of cookery came from my dad.

Also, Joseph and I used to breed rabbits and once, one of the baby rabbits came out not breathing. I will never forget the sadness on my brother Joseph's face. Just then, as Joseph's was trying to revive it, it suddenly came to life. This rabbit was to be my soulmate. I named him

Tufty, and he lived with me for months. I cried my eyes out when my old mo wanted us to get rid of them. Joseph fed wee Tufty back to health with a rubber eye dropper with hot water in it. Joseph loved animals too. He was so angry with Billy for all the cruelty he did to our pets.

Joseph, Vincent and Edward used to say that our three older brothers would all go to hell when they died, as they abused God's creatures and destroyed me. Although, as I said, Joseph, Vincent and Edward were my protectors when they could, they loved their wee sister. Dad taught me my music scales at the age of three, and then when I was five, I won my first award in the Regal House Cinema matinee club for kids on a Saturday morning. They gave the prize to the person whose name was shouted out the most.

Looking down, my three brothers were screaming, stamping their feet and shouting, "Sandra, Sandra, Sandra!" So I won. My dad was so proud of me and so were my three good brothers.

We were very poor, so I would pay at the kiosk then sneak down the front and let Joseph, Vincent and Edward in the side door. The film was always showed twice, so we stayed to watch it twice, stamping our feet at the cowboys and Indians, crying my eyes out at Bambi. I refuse to eat venison, as this just reminds me of Bambi not having a mother. I may be identifying with that one perhaps. I'm not veggie, or anything, I just seem to feel so sorry for a beautiful animal being killed for no reason. Nature at its best they say. I beg to differ, but that's just my perception of it. As a child, my love for animals was so great, as I saw them as God's creatures.

I loved cats. They used to say to me cats were for witches only, but that's just not true. My daughter has a cat today called Clover. Though Clover is very fat, she's beautiful and an elephant grey colour. If you saw a photograph of her from behind, you would think she was an elephant. She looks so funny.

The kids laugh, "Fat cat Clover."

This is only since she was dressed, as my daughter, the kids and my son-in-law-to-be don't overfeed her.

I look back at my life now and think of all the trauma, heartbreak and neglect I received as a child, and I just know this has made me person

I am today, and rightly so. I do like Sandra now. I am free to let all these little children, screaming inside of me, be brought out, nurtured and put back into their safe place. Little Sandra, an abused two-year-old right up until a 15-year-old, a survivor of starvation from a mother's eternal and maternal love, and a father who worshipped the ground I walked on. This book gives me closure on so many traumatic incidents. I could go on and on with the stories.

I also would love when I went apple picking as a child, as this would please my old mo again, as she'd say, "Good girl, Sandra, we can make a lovely apple pie," with the apples that were stolen from the trees down at the private, posh areas of Greenock like the Esplanade. Living off the land and surviving was so, so strong in me.

I also got bullied in school terribly and, to top it all off, I came home to also get a slap from my older brothers.

They told me that, "If you don't hit back if anyone hits you, you'll get slapped when you come home." So I did feel like I had been so hard done by. I always prayed as a little girl.

Being dyslexic, and schools not picking up

on this, was horrendous. I hated reading out in class 'cause I couldn't do it. My abuse in and outside the family home was to carry on into school. I would fall asleep in class and then get an occasional ruler slapped on your head.

"Harrison, wake up, you stupid, lazy girl."

I loved performing on stage. I got my first part in The Owl and The Pussycat production. I loved the acting and singing, but sadly neither my old mo nor my dad was in the audience to see me. This hurt when my wee classmates teased me and said that I had no mo or feather, as all their parents were there, but Sandra, as usual, was on her own.

The violence in the family home was to get worse when I was in primary school. There were times when I wondered who was going to be in for me after school. A latchkey kid they called me, only I had no key. Then again, I could always climb in the window, as I was so small.

I look back at my life and think, if there is a God, which I know there is today, how could he sit up on the big clouds above and watch this little girl, me, Wee Sandra, going through all this abuse and neglect? I thought God was on vacation sometimes. I always said my prayers at night. I would often pray for no one to come into my bedroom, or shout at me, and ask me to do thing sexual to them. Somehow it didn't work, so I just thought there was no God, and so I became a disbeliever and rebelled against everything and anything. Now I know that God was holding me in his arms and comforting me, as I went through this hell, as it was not God who abused me, it was human beings. I called them devils. I knew that satanism was ripping through this so-called family home. My brother Edward was like my big guardian angel. I was, and still am today, very close to my brothers that never hurt me. I know that somewhere along the lines that they protected me as much as they could. It was horrifying for my other brothers to find out the extent of their wee sister Sandra's abuse. They cried and hugged me when it all came out.

I am still today questioning why, why, why did my old mo allow this to happen to her only daughter, her baby girl, but I have to bring myself back into the day and think in survivor's mode as I am today, although I have Women's Aid still helping me, Rape Crisis, Colin at Sandyford – he's a tower of strength to me. He suggested, when my predators come into my nightmares, that I can shout for Colin and he will come into my dream with a baseball bat and, funnily enough, I called him in on a really bad nightmare last week. I shouted and shouted "Colin, Colin!" and in he came with a baseball bat with six-inch nails sticking out of the side. As soon as he appeared in my dream, my predators disappeared. I woke up feeling safe and secure. It really did work for me, this technique, so I sat up in bed for a while, to gather my thoughts, and then lay down and drifted into a deep sleep with no fear. Thanks for that Colin from Sandyford. I see Colin again next week for my final session with him. I'm sad that I won't see him again, but I know I can call on him any time and he'd be there. He's the best psychologist I have ever had in my entire life of counselling is Colin MacKillop of Sandyford Clinic, Glasgow.

Val from Women's Aid is another of my guardian angels, who helps me still today, and has been on my journey with me. She knows the horror of these little, damaged children inside me, who are: Sandra Harrison, the two-year-old, raped, abused, put in a dustbin with hot ashes and left to die, and Wee Sandra with the measles, a four-year-old being abused while I was sick, then Wee Sanny, the six-year-old, constantly being abused, called a liar and slapped, to the Wee Sandra bride making her first Holy Communion, confessing her sins as she thought she should and given penance, 10 Our Fathers and 10 Hail Marys, for letting them abuse me, then that little white bridal outfit, borrowed from a neighbour, used to make my predators give me money for my old mo, Sadie. I felt as if I was a child prostitute being sent out to the wolves.

Now, as I pass Ravenscraig Hospital, I see they have demolished the old hospital, but I can still see the path, at the railway line, that I had to hold on to while one of my predators was threatening to throw me under the passing train if I told anyone what he'd made me do. I hate it when anyone calls me Wee Sanny today, as that was his name for me and, funnily enough, I was down at a retreat in Girvan called Trochrague Guest House, run by the Jericho Brothers, and there was another girl in there called Sandra and she kept calling me Wee Sanny. I knew this was a big trigger for me, but I didn't have the heart to tell her to stop calling me that name, as she wouldn't have known, so I just prayed to my god of understanding, my supreme being, to help me change my thinking, remove my fear and accept Wee Sanny as the name she called me without triggering me or discussing why not to call me that. It's easier to smile and accept it nowadays.

These little Sandras are all part of me. At the moment, I can't seem to get them all together and put them to bed; that would be massive closure for me. I do know that day will come, when I will have this closure, until then the Wee Sandras have a bit of a journey to go through. As the trauma team get started on my traumatic past, the more I can bring these little Sandras to the fore and set them free, to fly safely like little angels. I do hope that day will come soon, as it's so hard to have all these kids screaming inside me to get out, even the 13-year-old. She was called that Sandra Harrison by another predator. He waited, filled me with alcohol, and then abused me. He is now dead. Then there was the 15-year-old, well 14 or 15, Oor Sandra.

My predator then said, "Oh, I'm sorry. I

thought you were my wife."

"Er no, I'm your sister, you sick, sick man." Only to get battered, two black eyes and have to sing on stage wearing sunglasses in the winter, saying that I was a Roy Orbison tribute.

Singing is still my passion today, and the acting, as it takes me away from me, if you can understand what I mean, as I'm in character, and I do use this to my advantage, using my God-given gift of music and acting to shield the wee broken girls that still live inside me. My son and daughter have been a tower of strength to me through all this mess, and it's hard for them to think about how badly I was treated as a child.

I sit in hope and pray the CID get the other paedophiles that I have told them about and take them to court, and also make them face truth about how they affected my whole life. Even bringing up my kids, I thought every man was an predator of children, so I inflicted that fear on to my kids at a very early age. It is not healthy for me or them. I know fear can be your worst enemy, but it also can be the best defence you'll ever have. It's human emotions. It's hard at times to cope with these emotions, but somehow, deep down, I got the strength and courage to write this book, a horrific story of an innocent child that was so groomed, from the age of two until the age of 15, with years and years of sexual abuse, being raped, incest, prostituted out to the beast by an old mother that said she loved me.

"You're a good girl, Sandra. This is our little secret. No one can find out what happened to Sandra." What happened in the houses 3 and 4 Stafford Road stayed in these houses.

Looking back, I can tell I was in so much fear for my life. They destroyed my childhood, they robbed me of any self-worth I had, sexually abused me, all 23 of them, and then threw me aside like a piece of dirt just taken from their shoe. My first drink of alcohol helped me cope with all of this until I could not stop drinking, and I was desperate. My trusted fellowship nurtured me back to sobriety. My biological father, Wee Johnny, stopped drinking when I did. He was the best dad in the whole world to me. He worshipped the ground I walked on, and I made my father a solemn promise to keep sober, keep sober-minded people all around me and then I'd have a life beyond my wildest dreams, which I do have today.

My husband, of 15 years now, gave me the courage to lift that phone, call Police Scotland and tell them exactly everything I knew about the poor Margaret Fleming case and my abuse over the years. They are very similar, although Margaret is gone. They murdered her and would have done the same to me if I hadn't had all my security and my big husband to look after me, keeping me strong. I will forever be in his debt. Children are innocent and should never ever have a life like Sandra's. I really do like myself today. I am me and you are you. Well I do say, you be you, and I'll be me.

Well I sit here, in Crown House, a place of safety, with my son who I could cry for, as my past trauma has seriously affected my son. I am so worried about him. His mental state is not a great; trauma, trauma, trauma. It's horrendous trying to live a normal life in abnormal circumstances. I thank God today that I never took my own life when I was 15. I continually tried to harm myself by cutting, well slitting, my wrists open and hoping I could bleed the poison the beasts put into me out. I was screaming out for the help I needed as a child, but instead I only got battered, thrown against a wall in my bedroom and told that I did that because I was drunk. Well no, 'cause the next time I was sober. So they never heard my cries and screams for the attention I was seeking, as I really wanted my abuse to stop but I didn't know how to stop it.

I've played the victim for years.

"You'd drink if you had a life like mine," I'd say, going to the extent of putting the vodka into my mouth and thinking all my past would just disappear into thin air, but no. I was to wake up lying on a cemetery grave, trying to make deals with God that I'd stick to half pints of lager and lime and only drink on a Friday or Saturday. By that time of my life's path, shall we call it, the alcohol was my crutch. I didn't know how to stop. I was so full of fear about stopping, as I would have to face up to all that traumatic sexual and physical abuse suffered as a child. I manage then to crawl home, on my hands and knees, crying, got to my front door, only to fall over a book. It was the Yellow Pages, a phone directory, and there it was in black, bold writing AA – Alcoholics Anonymous, so I picked up the phone and my life started then, the 25th of March, year 2000, my sobriety birthday.

Up to today, I have not wanted or needed alcohol. I believe in God, I meditate, I pray, I go to my lovely Baptist church on a Sunday, I also help out with the children's ministry, and I love it. I'm starting to get the Sandra back that I knew and loved. I try my best to help anyone who has had struggles in life, especially sexual or physical abuse. I can help a lot of people, so I think this is my calling, as I am such a strong person today. I can see beyond human behaviours and be on a great spiritual path, clean and positive, the way God made me. This may sound strange, but I actually wouldn't change a thing about my past. Only I have to stop beating myself up for the works of the beast implanted in me, from the time when I was that innocent child, Wee Sandra, the wain, of two years old until 15 years old when I started to say no, no, no, no more. I will not do this to you, and you will not touch me again. After a few kickings, like running through a gauntlet, getting kicked, spat on, punched and humiliated, I still knew I would survive this mess of a life I had. I still can't forgive my old mo but, like an elephant, I can't forget, so it's not easy letting go.

I sing still and love it. I probably will never get the chance to be rich and famous but, the thing is, I have a God-given gift of my voice, and I'm going to pass this on and share it with as many people as I can, and who I can help, till the day I die. I will hold my hands and arms open to anyone who I can help, as I reckon that's God's plan for me. Christmas comes, and I want to bring smiles to faces, joy and peace to the people who need it. Keep the children safe, I say, and protect them all from the predators, beasts and paedophiles of this world. I will now gladly go and entertain in the community for the community, this is the person I have become, caring, loving and funny. People like me and, most importantly, I like me. My past has made my future. I thank God each day for helping me survive all this trauma, and I pray deeply for all the lost, suffering victims in the world. I do hope they live a positive, good, clean life as I do and not stay in that hell they have been in. I am so blessed today being a survivor of 23 predators. I can't believe I survived all those years of neglect and abuse. I also have really happy memories with my close siblings and this time of the year, Christmas, I remember carol-singing and cleaning paths for older people so they could walk out of their doors, only sometimes I would not have any salt to put down, so if the path froze over it wasn't very safe but, hey, I was a child working hard to provide for food for the family.

I did used to keep a couple of pennies back for a caramel for myself. I love the Scottish, dairy caramels. You chewed it forever and when you'd finished you'd lick the rest from the paper. I never had the privilege to get fruit as a child – we just couldn't afford it, simple as that – so fruit was a great treat for me. Thank God it's not like that today. I love my fruit and the fact that I don't have to pick berries off jaggy trees and prick my fingers so much that they bleed any more, but I did learn at an early age how to make jam, raspberry and blackberry jam, so there is a positive result from that.

I always remember when my predators groomed me, they all had different techniques. Some would show me a Page Three picture of a girl from a newspaper. One of my predators asked me if I had one of them, pointing to her bottom.

I said yes, then he asked me "Can I see it?" 'cause he didn't believe I had one. Then, after weeks and weeks of going into that house, he would ask to see my bum. He never touched me at first but, as the weeks went on, he did. I remember this particular predator giving me money after he touched me. It was always his smelly, smokey fingers I could remember and them being so rough on my front bum, rubbing it so hard, I had tears running down my face.

"What you greeting fur?" he'd say. "No if I hit or punched you, then you should greet [which means cry in Scotland], but I haven't done that, so just be a good girl." I always wanted to be a good girl so I did what he said, but then I hated going to that house, yet for reasons I was sent there for them to look after me. I got so used to holding a man's erect penis in my hand by the age of seven years old, as I was taught very young how to hold it, squeeze it and make them smile. It was all so sick. I was told by all of my predators that no one would believe me and they would all call me a dirty, clatty, wee bastard.

One of my predators used to make me wash my bum so hard with soap that it would sting me, then he'd tell me I wasn't doing it properly, and he'd do it using his big, rough, adult hands on my private parts and this was so sore after my ordeal, I would just get passed on to the others. It was funny how they all knew each other; so coincidental.

My whole life as a child was abuse, torture and neglect. I got so used to the sexual abuse, I always knew what was coming next or who I was getting arranged to be with.

One of my predators once said, "You know what we all say at our wee meetings? Go for Wee Sandra, she's the easiest one to get hold of and she'll never tell." You see, I was told they would kill me if I told anyone what was happening to me. I even believed it when they told me I asked for it, wearing wee, short school skirts, which I always tried to pull down to below my knees, and my knee-high socks. It was all my fault, and I believed it was. I remember, well, never shall I forget, the pain I was in through my private parts being so raw and my bum hurting so badly. I would scream into my pillow after the abuse, it was like a silent scream, as I didn't want anyone to know the pain was so bad. I wanted to die. I used to ask God why I was born, why people hurt me so much and why I was always a bad, little girl. That's what was programmed into my mind, you see, from the age of four. I was a very bad girl for letting my predators be turned on, I asked for it. Such an innocent child, I was a victim of their sick, sick minds. I started to feel relief when I cut my wrists, as I honestly wanted to bleed to death, but always one of my predators would find me – you see, they were all around me, I couldn't escape – then I would end up in casualty getting stitched up as usual. Never once did the doctors ask if I'd done this myself, as my predators would say that I fell on to glass.

At one stage of my life, I wanted to be in a children's home, and when I said that to my old mo she said, "They beat you up with sticks and lock you in a room and keep you in this dark room for days," so that terrified me, as I was so scared of the dark.

I remember getting my period at the age of 13. I was sent home from school, as I fainted. The teacher ran me home. My dad was in, so I told him what had happened. My dad made a bed on the couch for me and went to the shops, bought me sanitary towels, told me to go and wash and keep changing them every so often, and this would go away in a few days. I trusted my dad so much, I loved him with all my heart, and I knew he would never hurt me. I begged him not to tell my mother, as she scared the hell out of me when she told me this would happen when I became a woman. I was only 13 and certainly didn't feel like a woman, I was still a wee girl. My older brother came into my room that very night to abuse me, and I told him I had started my periods. He wasn't happy at all.

"That's all we need now," he said. "I need to let everyone know." I was so embarrassed.

I cried and said, "I don't want anyone to know."

He said, "You stupid, wee girl. This changes everything now, you know." I didn't understand what he meant, but I found out later on they wouldn't touch me when I had my periods. This was to my advantage, because my predators couldn't touch me or hurt me when I was on my period, but that never stopped them making me touch them, or sucking their erect penis, which only took half the embarrassment and shame from me. I would lie always and say I was on my period so they wouldn't touch me. I wasn't allowed boyfriends, they made sure of that.

My first boyfriend was when I was 15, and it was a secret until my older brother found out, and he battered me into a pulp. I was so bruised and battered, that I had to lie in bed for days.

My second boyfriend was warned, "If you touch my sister, I'll kill you." So this boy was more like a best friend than a boyfriend, and the relationship phased out. I was so scared to let anyone in to see the real me. I was always acting as someone else, still singing and loving the stage, and the applause of the audience liking me was the best feeling in the world. I felt someone loved me, my audience, and I never wanted the bright lights and the buzz of the music and stage to end, but when it did the abuse would start. Now my predators owned me. I was their little toy to pass around, and it made it a hundred times worse when it was your brother and no one would believe me, as I was told would be the case.

My first love came along. His sister was my

best friend and sang in the band with us. We got engaged, I lost my virginity at 16½, and so did he. I was besotted with this guy, but I was told no boyfriends or you're out of the band. I was so much in love with this boy, I chucked in the band, which was bad for me, as my whole family fell out with me, and I was told I was giving up my whole future for a boy. It didn't help matters that my manager was lesbian and her partner, well one of them, at the time tried to lure me into being gay, which I always knew I wasn't, so I had a break from the band. That's when my relationship crumbled, as I only had my boyfriend. Now we were seeing each other every day, my love became an obsession for me. I was so possessive that boy couldn't move, or even talk to anyone else, without me accusing him of having an affair, which was not true, just a symptom of all this distrust in my head. Then one night, he told me one of my predators tried to touch him up, and he got scared and ran away. That was the ruination of that relationship, and it ended not long after this. I was heartbroken. He was my safety net, my soulmate, now I had nothing.

By this time I was 20 years old and had moved out of the family home, which I called the House of Horrors, and had moved across the water, leaving the waitressing job I had, to go to a big hotel. I was free. That's when I started drinking alcohol big time, and by the age of 21 I was a full-blown alcoholic, as the alcohol blocked out all my traumatic past, gave me the bravado to fight back and gave my predators all their characters. I had become a big threat to them, but I never feared them. I realized that as soon as I mentioned the police to them, they crumbled and stayed away from me.

Then I started a career as a bar manager, in this big hotel, and started singing and writing songs again. All the big bands from Glasgow would come to this hotel, and I sang with them all. I loved it. Then the big shock came, the hotel was going into bankruptcy, and we were all out of work. I was homeless, as I stayed in the hotel, so I had to go back to the House of Horrors again, with the violence and police presence nearly every night, as my family would constantly fight, not just fists, weapons, hammers, knives, it was back to hell for me.

I got my job back waitressing and was to meet a boy who drank the same as me and was a binge drinker. I thought this was the man of my dreams, we had so much in common and that was alcoholism. I left my job as a waitress and became a professional singer with what was called the Inverclyde Roadshow, another great band. I sang night and day in hospitals, residential homes, schools and community centres. I loved this so much, and then I got engaged again, to my new boyfriend, and I fell pregnant.

I was singing in a mental hospital one day, and a patient attacked me. I ended up in hospital and lost a baby, but the amazing thing was that it was a twin, and the other baby survived and was still safe inside me when I was discharged from hospital. The whole time, I had my brother Joseph by my side, holding my hand. Me and Frank were very close. Like twins, we felt each other's pain. I still love and trust him with all my heart, and also my two other brothers, we were all similar in age and all musical.

Discharged, I was now planning a wedding. I still kept my secret about my abuse well hidden from everyone, and I was also still getting threatened about being battered and killed if I let the big secret out; I still lived in fear. The marriage went through, and then along came the most beautiful girl in the world, my daughter. I just loved her so much. I wasn't going to let any monsters harm her.

We moved to a small village not far from where I lived but far enough to keep the wolves away from the door. Many a day, I would walk along the estate, not far from our wee one-bedroomed flat, watching the horses, sheep and other wildlife with the lovely sound of birds singing, and the peace I had away from the troubled home I had left was amazing. I was a new mum with my beautiful daughter, who I protected, although I was very insecure. I kept a net over her pram, so no one outside could look in and gloat as, by this time, I trusted no one, and I said I would kill anyone who tried to touch my daughter. I was so insecure and afraid, that I started suffering from postnatal depression. This was when I first came out about parts of my childhood. I told my then husband that I had been sexually abused as a child. He didn't take this well and went out and got really pissed drunk, leaving me with my wee baby girl and all my fears on my own in the flat. I was terrified. I just cuddled my wee baby girl and told her she would be safe as long as I lived.

I couldn't deal with my past coming back, although I told my then husband that there was only one predator. I couldn't tell him there were many more, as I thought he'd hate me, and I would be that wee child slut they'd called me. I decided to stop breastfeeding my daughter, as I wanted to get intoxicated with the alcohol again to blot it all out, so I did. The thing was I still wanted my daughter to get breast milk, so I came up with an idea to buy a breast pump so I could express my milk, keep it in the fridge and hit the booze for a few days. Better still, I bought two, so I would be pumping like a big coo for hours for the sake of getting out of my face drunk to blot my horrific past out. This carried on, and two alcoholic parents living under one roof was toxic. Three years later, I fell pregnant again and give birth to a gorgeous little boy. My family was made, and I was in my glory. I sheltered my kids as much as I could, as I didn't want them to be harmed at all. I wanted them to be safe and never to experience the childhood I had; no child should have to suffer that horrendous life. My whole mission in life was the safety of my kids, and other kids too, but I still couldn't open up completely about my horrifying past.

After my son was born, we decided one bedroom was not big enough, so we looked for another, bigger house, though it still had to be in the village, as this was my wee safe place. Sometimes we would get the odd visit from my family members, and because my husband didn't know they were part of the ring, I was on my guard all the time, protecting my kids. I loved my bigger house, and now we had a horse that I bought for my daughter called Ginty. Drink became too important, debt got higher and Ginty got sold. I'll never forget the look of sadness on my daughter's face as we sold her. My son was too young to understand, but my daughter was heartbroken.

We stayed in this lovely, wee village for as long as we could but, not with my approval, the house got sold. We moved our belongings to a house in a wild housing scheme near my family, which I hated, though I kept the children in the same village school. The marriage got really toxic and violent, on both ends. I went to a Women's Aid refuge and, from that day, my life started to change. Women's Aid brought a whole lot of demons out of me, but I was still in denial.

We tried to resume the broken marriage a few times, but it never worked. I had stopped singing completely and was on my own with my two kids. I got a bigger house, which I still live in today. The kids were turning into teenagers, and this is when it hit home, I had a serious drink problem, as I couldn't stop drinking and I desperately wanted to.

After my last drink, I was to wake up in a cemetery, clutching a bottle of empty vodka, trying to make deals with God, saying, "If you help me out of this one Lord, I will only drink half pints of lager."

I was desperate to stop drinking. Drink had destroyed me inside and out. I had no friends, and my family had disowned me. I was nothing. I was back to being the wee, scared, abused girl I was when I was a kid. Suddenly, I stood up, crawled home, fell in through the door and fell over a Yellow Pages, which opened at the first page, and staring me in the face was AA, Alcoholics

Anonymous. So I plucked up the courage and lifted the phone. Within 20 minutes, two AA members were at my door, and I invited them in.

I said, "I can't stop drinking, and I'm desperate to do so." Just then, the lovely man and woman started telling me their stories, and I could identify with every single word, it was as if they knew my life. They asked me to go to a meeting with them that night. I couldn't, I was still shaking, but promised I'd go to the next day's meeting, which I did, and my happy journey began. I got stuck into AA, and I was now determined never to drink again. They told me I'd have a life beyond my wildest dreams and that all came true.

I was to meet my second husband who totally adored me and I him. We went to Australia, where I'd always dreamed of going as a child, and I met my three sisters who I'd not seen in years. They arranged all our wedding for us. It was the happiest time of my life. We stayed in Australia for nine weeks, came home and had a big second reception in the town hall in Greenock for the families. There my son gave me away, well walked me to my blessing, and my daughter was my bridesmaid along with her best friend and my niece, and my husband's brother was the best man. My new, wonderful life had begun.

The two years before our marriage, I lost the most important man in my life, my wee daddy. That broke my heart. I didn't think I would ever get over it. I looked after him, as much as I could, until he was finished. He begged me to let him go. I was holding his hand and kissing his head when he took his last breath. A big smile came over him, and he was at peace. I'm so glad my dad didn't know about the extent of my abuse, as it would have killed him long before then.

The funeral was so sad. I don't know where I got the courage, but I went up and sang 'Danny Boy' in front of the whole load of people who had come, and I never broke down, as my father's words were still ringing in my ears. "Never let your emotions get in the way of your performance." The congregation erupted with applause after I sang.

When the funeral was over my soon-to-be husband stayed by my side for weeks and comforted me in my deep, deep grief. Then plans for the Australian wedding followed. We were met by my Australian family at the airport and that was definitely a life beyond my wildest dreams. We toured Australia and had a ball, came home as Mr. and Mrs. and we built a beautiful life between us. That was 15 years ago today.

Marriage was great. My son and daughter moved out and got their own homes and kids. Now we have five grandkids, four girls and one boy. We started to travel the world, my husband and I, and I loved it. I went back to my singing, which is even better now than before, and my husband has stood by me and protected me through it all. I still love him dearly.

Years down the line, an article appeared in the Greenock Telegraph showing a house and asked the key question about whether readers knew this special needs girl who had been missing and not seen from 1998 to 1999, a long time. At first I couldn't think. My daughter phoned and sent me the picture of the house, just outside the small village we stayed in. I recognized the house right away and told my daughter what I knew about it. She suggested I called 101 Police Scotland and told them everything I knew. Well I did. Soon CID officers from Govan were in my house and asked me what I knew about the case, so I told them all I knew.

A CID officer said, "What makes you think they harmed her?"

That's when I broke my anonymity about staying silent. I said, "Because they were supposed to be caring for Margaret. My oldest brother as well." The CID officer asked again why I thought Margaret was abused, and my reply was, "Because they did it to me, and that was one of the houses they tried to take me into."

Now my secret was out I cried and cried. I told the CID officers all I knew about Margaret Fleming, that she was a special needs girl whose mum and dad had split up, and that Margaret lived with her dad until her dad died. Her dad knew the two carers, who are in jail now, and also my older brother knew of him, as my brother was also close friends of the carers. Well, I started to explain what I knew about this girl that had not been seen for 20 years or more.

The tall ships had come to Greenock, and I was still performing alcoholically. I'd decided to pay my brother a visit and confront him about all the abuse he had done to me from the age of four to 15 years old. I wanted to know why he'd done this to me, and why he'd passed me around to all the other 22 or more paedophiles. He'd denied this of course. He said that he didn't know about the others that had abused me well. This was a lie, as I remembered back, years ago, he could tell me exactly who abused me, where it was and how much money, sweets and presents they gave me for what I was told to do with them. I'd had a drink in me, got very angry and started to shout and bawl at him. Then his partner came out of her bedroom and asked what was going on. He pleaded in my ear not to mention it to her, and then he asked her to pour me a drink, as I was just going through a hard time. So after about five minutes, she came back in the room with a very strong, tall glass of Bacardi and Coke, and I sat and sipped away.

At one point, I went to use the toilet. When I came back out, I finished the rest of the drink. I started to sober up really quick then, I was on this high and didn't feel angry or sad, just wide awake and wanting to party.

I said, "What kind of Bacardi was that?"

My brother's reply was, "Oh, we put

something in it to cheer you up. It's called speed. It's fine. It only takes all your worries away and makes you wanna dance and stay awake," which it did, only now and again I felt like I had passed out then was wide awake again.

My brother got me to one side and held me tight.

He said, "You'll always be mine. I own you, so just forget about the daft stories of your past." Then another drink appeared.

I couldn't tell you what else happened that night, I just had vivid memories of him trying to get me to walk into this cottage on a beach to meet his friends, the carers, and that was why I'd noticed the house in the local paper, asking if anyone knew who'd lived there and their names. By the grace of God, I fought my way out of going into that house; I could sense that something didn't sit right.

As I woke up on my brother and his partner's couch, in their living room, I was ill and felt so, so sick. When the two of them came in the living room, my brother and his partner, she handed me a glass of water and a pill. I was so sick, I would have taken anything to calm my stomach down and, knowing she was a nurse, I trusted her. I swallowed the pill then, after about 10 minutes, I felt great. My brother told me we were going out in his boat to Greenock, to see the tall ships, and another drink appeared. I drank this too and began to feel that high again and, as I heard the two of them laughing at me, I just knew they'd spiked my drink again. Going in and out of consciousness, I remember his partner taking my blood pressure and checking my pulse.

I could hear her say, "She's fine. Let's take her out in the boat to the tall ships." So the next thing I remember I was in my brother's boat, passing the house they'd tried to take me into the previous night.

"That's our friend's house. I really wanted you to meet them. You could have stayed there last night, Sandra. You let me down not going in," he said, and I felt bad because I'd let them down, not knowing this could have been another one of his sick games like he did to me as a child, as I was full of drink and whatever drugs they'd spiked me with.

So off we went to Greenock. I only remember them speaking about the importance of them trying to have a child. This set off alarm bells in my head, as both of them said they were going to adopt or go for IVF treatment. I did find out later on that they'd tried to buy children, well unborn children, from family and friends that were pregnant. Everyone feared this man, my brother, so much that no one would tell the authorities anything that was going on, and my old mo just agreed with everything they did and said.

After the tall ships day I went home, as I felt worse and couldn't take any more of the concoctions they'd given me. I got home, and I telephoned the doctor. When he came out to visit me, I froze and couldn't tell him what had happened the night before, so I just put it down to too much wine 'cause the tall ships were in and I was partying. My whole body was shaking, my head was thumping, and I couldn't stop being sick. I had never felt as bad as that in my whole life. I thought I was going to die and, as my kids were staying with their friends, I was on my own in my room with complete fear and some tablets from the doctor to help me stop being sick. I fell in and out of sleep, my whole life passing in front of my eyes. My childhood abuse was so real now, what they'd all done to me came rushing back, and I remembered the pain in my bum as a child and me screaming into a pillow, or trying my best to fight my predators off. They did the very same, well two of them did, as my brother had done the previous night and that was drug me. Then I suddenly remembered getting a cloth put over my mouth at the age of 10 and whatever was on that cloth knocked me out, the same feeling I was having right then. I remembered being beaten to a pulp, being horrifically, sexually abused, then being told I was a very special little girl to them and only they loved, me no one else, and then the slap from my old mo.

"Liar, liar, liar!" she yelled.

That night, after the tall ships, I'd wished I was dead. I cried and cried, like I've never cried before, it was hell on earth.

I explained all this to the CID officers that were in my house, then I told them that someone in the year 1999 asked me to ask my older brother and his partner what had happened to the special needs girl that the two of them, and their two friends that stayed in that cottage, were caring for, as they'd said that the gypsies had stolen her away. Now I do know it was one of my other brothers who'd asked me to ask him. This was in my old mo's house, so I walked into the living room, and my old mo was sitting in her usual position on the couch laughing and joking with my brother and his partner.

I asked, "What happened to this special needs girl yous were all supposed to be looking after and the gypsies stole her?" I was angry when I asked, as my hatred for all the people in that room that day was at its peak.

My brother launched at me, grabbed me by the throat, pushed me against the wall and shouted, "Who told you that? How do you know about Margaret Fleming? That's a job that was done by [he named the other so-called carers]." When I asked him this question, his face turned grey, and he was so, so angry.

His partner also shouted, "How did she know about Margaret, John? Who told her?"

The fear was ripping through my whole body. I could smell a rat. I knew somehow something was not right, and I said, "You two couldn't even look after yourselves."

At this time, I was at the end of my so-called

drinking career, so I was shaking and feeling sick to the core, but I will never forget the expressions on my brother's and his partner's faces when I mentioned a special needs girl. I didn't even know the girl's name. It was my brother's partner who'd said her name was Margaret. He kept shouting and shouting at me, and this brought memories of me as a wee child right back. I was getting battered and shouted at by him from a very young age, and my other predators used to threaten and shout at me too.

I felt so alone. No one in the house came to my rescue. I was once again in my life fed to the wolves. I felt my legs shaking, the whole atmosphere of my old mo's living room was frightening, like a horror movie, and it took me right back to my past. I couldn't say who'd told me to go in and ask the question about Margaret. In fact, I didn't want to tell him it was my other brother who'd told me to ask, as I knew my oldest brother would have battered him.

I couldn't breathe, and my old mo was shouting, "Argh, just leave her alone. She knows nothing." So he dropped me to the floor like a bundle of unwanted rags.

When I got up, I ran and kept running, never stopping until I got to my own house. And then I remembered the words once again.

My brother had said, "I will kill you if you mention that ever again."

Then one of the CID officers asked if I had anything else to say, and I told them, "I'm pretty sure my brother had something to do with Margaret's murder." The CID girls were really nice and understanding.

They said, "Sandra, we will have to come back and speak to you because this is a very high-profile case, and now you have opened up about your childhood sexual abuse this makes this a lot worse."

I broke down in floods of tears and asked, if possible, if I could have my friend Helen with me at the next interview, as I knew if my husband heard it all he would crack and not be able to handle it, as he had only recently found out about the whole story. He was gutted and angry to discover the life his wife had suffered as a child, and he hated paedophiles. He called them the scum of the earth.

"Children should be protected," he'd say.

If it wasn't for my husband, I would have definitely died from this secret life I led.

The CID officers left. They said Victim Support, Women's Aid, Rape Crisis and court officials would start to get in touch with me. Now there was no way back for me. I was more interested in Police Scotland finding out exactly what had happened to Margaret. While all this investigation was going on, everyone who had known about my brother's involvement with a massive paedophile ring and the knowledge of a special needs girl's disappearance kept quiet, except one of my other brothers, who I trusted and still do, told all he knew about the missing Margaret. My other family members started acting so strangely towards me, as if they hated me for telling my secret and were still in total denial.

"Sandra, my wee sister, she can tell more stories and lies more than anyone we know," I was told they'd said.

Now I'm not a Harrison at all, I am very proud to be a McMenamin. I did promise my father I'd keep my biological name, Sandra Harrison, for my singing and acting, so I have kept to his wishes, only for my dad, no one else.

The court case of the special needs girl's murder and my historical sexual abuse case ran together. I so wanted the CID to jail all my predators, some of who still walk the streets today, but the case stays open for the others, and they're still seeking more people to come forward and report them. Unfortunately, some of the witnesses are dead now, my nieces and David, all because of the coping mechanisms they used like drugs. It's these things that kill you, and in the end, speaking up is the only way to find your freedom from everything like that.

I got all my help from the authorities the CID directed to me and the strength of my husband, or I wouldn't have had the energy to go through with it, along with my close friends, Helen and Mandy, and all my AA women supporters who are still there today for me.

I had to tell my kids, who are now adults, the extremes of my abuse. My daughter hasn't taken it so well, I do worry about her, whereas my son has a bit more strength and does make me cry if I want to get angry. If I want to speak out and I want the same support with my husband, there are still some tortures I cannot speak about but more counselling time will get me that closure.

My counsellor Colin was an angel in disguise for me. He took me right back to the age of four and worked on all these different wee children who were inside me, suffering. I had to deal with them one by one, the kids within me from ages four to 15. It was so hard, as even now I can't put these little girls into me, a woman, I can't see they are me. Maybe distancing myself from these little Sandras does help me cope with what happened, along with my music and entertaining.

There are three brothers who I love dearly, as they never hurt me the way the older ones did. My sisters in Australia are still trying to deal with things, so there's not much contact there at moment, as they had a different mother to me. I had an evil witch that never wanted me to begin with, while they didn't have that woman around when they were small.

As the court cases drew near, my counselling stepped up. Colin was my rock and Val, from Women's Aid, was my angel. They found Margaret's two carers trying to flee to London at Glasgow train station and arrested them.

They also arrested my older brother and, as the murder case was high profile, they got all the witnesses they needed to come and give evidence about Margaret. You see, the carers pretended Margaret was still alive, and they were cashing her DLA sickness money for all the years she wasn't there, making a sum of approximately £80,000. There was also a young man who was Margaret's boyfriend, set up by my older brother. I assumed it was to get the two of them a child. This boy was to be called at a high court but, unfortunately, he was found dead in his house two days before he was called. Coincidence, I thought at first. My older brother denied even knowing the two other carers until his partner got called up to the stand. She told the court they both knew them and also this other boy that was going out with Margaret. She said they put a stop to it because Margaret, being special needs, she didn't think it was an appropriate relationship.

Bullshit, went through my mind when I read that statement. The lies were unreal that flowed from all their mouths. The carers got out on bail and that led to a television programme interviewing them, asking all about Margaret

Fleming, the gangmaster and drug dealer. They said she ran away as soon as the police came to the house to ask if she was there, as a social worker had appeared to ask how Margaret was and had felt something was wrong. The police enquiries found that she was last seen in 1999, this was the same year that I'd asked my older brother about them looking after the special needs girl. As I think back, maybe I should have gone into that cottage all those years ago, as I could have possibly saved Margaret or noticed that something was wrong if she'd been still alive then. I don't think we will ever get the full truth.

The cases of the murder and my sexual abuse ran on the same week. Val took me up to the high court, and Val was also there when I saw one of my predators and the murderers. I nearly lost it, and Val had to calm me down and take me into the witness room, where I was told not to leave. I did feel, at one point, that I was the accused, as they could walk freely through the court and I couldn't. I was more at ease when I noticed two of my childhood friends, both male, who had also opened up and spoken about what my brother had done to them. Then I found out from the procurator fiscal that eight other children, now adults, had come forward. I no longer felt alone – what a weight off my shoulders.

When I saw my brother downstairs in court, he was wearing the usual black coat that he wore when he was at court and jeans. He still looked like a dirty, old man, and his partner was by his side acting as if she knew nothing.

"I can assure you, Val," I said, "she's in on it. I bet my life on that."

That day, I never got called up and was sent away to appear in a couple of days time. While I drove down the road in Val's car, I was still shaking with nerves, as the thought of a jury and all the other officials hearing my horrendous story really got to me. I felt embarrassed, alone and very, very sad. I didn't sleep that night. The doctor was called to give me a sleeping pill, as my head was racing and my husband was worried sick about me.

Next day, I woke up to news stating that Margaret Fleming's two carers had been found guilty of murder and a lot of other charges of abuse, neglect and lying regarding Margaret's whereabouts, knowing that for all these years she was dead, as they'd killed her. I was so happy when I found that news out, it was a worldwide story, and then I didn't have to give evidence on the case, as they'd been found guilty and sent to jail.

Then the next day came, and I had to go up again to the high court to be a witness against my older brother in connection with how he'd brutally beaten me up and sexually abused me, along with a paedophile ring of 23 men that I could remember. I sat in the waiting room, trembling, and that wee child came back. I felt a wee, innocent child again that had done something wrong. Val kept reassuring me that it would be fine. My minister's wife had given me a little oak cross, which I clutched so hard, and prayed as I've never prayed before. Then the court official came into the room to call me into court. I had to walk a very long trek, with my head down, as I had to pass jury members, and I couldn't have eye contact with anyone. This was the most frightening thing I had experienced. I still didn't feel like I was the victim, I felt like I was the one who had done wrong. This, I now know, goes back to all my predators mind controlling me, grooming me, and then making me feel it was my fault. I was asking for it, they'd say. Now I walked through what felt like a gauntlet, shaking and clutching my small wooden cross.

I got to the witness stand. I looked at the jury, and all these faces were fixed on me. A glass shielded partition separated me from my brother, I couldn't bear to see him, and then court began. My advocate started asking me questions. I thought about the question and answered it in the most truthful way I could. There was no hesitation, as I knew the truth and that's all I needed to say. Then followed the devil's advocate, as I called him, my brother's defence. I was told before court that I wasn't to mention any other predators, or the murder trial, it was only about me and what my brother had done to me. He asked me lots of questions, which I answered yes or no, I didn't elaborate on any of them.

Then he asked me something in the following way: "Mrs. McMenamin, you telephoned Police Scotland to tell them your brother had sexually abused you when you were a child."

I said, "No, I didn't."

He said, "Oh, yes you did. I have it here in

front of me."

I replied, "I telephoned Police Scotland about the information I knew regarding the Margaret Fleming murder case and how my brother was involved."

Straight away they reset the court, obviously not expecting that answer. So I was sent back to the waiting room, with Val, for about 10 minutes which felt like an hour. Then I was called to court again. Now, once again, I was stood in front of the jury and the devil's advocate. They showed me pictures of my brother to identify him, which I did. That was the first time I broke down, as I thought I was the big, bad wolf sending my brother to jail and still blaming myself. Then, after a few other questions, the big question came.

"Now," said the devil's advocate, "this house, the family home you lived in with 10 siblings and parents, must have been very busy and you were the youngest of them all. Are you stating that no one saw or heard anything strange coming from your bedroom or any other room in the house?"

"Oh yes, it was very busy," I said, "but they were abusing me also, sir, but I was told not to mention other names, as their cases have not been called yet. I was only to tell you what my older brother did."

Then I saw my brother's defence lawyer looking at mine and saying, "There's more?" And my lawyer showed him a folder which must have contained the other predators inside it. Well that was certainly a court stopper. The court was recessed again, and it was back to the witness room for me and Val, only this time it seemed to be longer than before. Val said I'd answered properly and now the court was having a major discussion about my case. I started to feel things were going my way, and I would be free very soon from all of it. Then the court liaison came in and called me back up to the witness box. Still clutching my little cross, I got asked several other questions by my brother's QC and answered them the only way I knew how, with the truth.

Then that magic phrase materialised. "No more questions, Your Honour."

The judge looked at me, thanked me and said, "That will be all now, Mrs. McMenamin. You're free to go."

The word free hit me like a ton of bricks, I

really did feel free. I couldn't wait to leave that court, but the court liaison suggested we hang back for the accused to go so I wouldn't have to bump into them. So we sat, had a coffee and a sandwich, and then headed off in Val's car down the motorway.

I felt, at this time, sort of numb, as if I'd had to relive my horrendous childhood again, and go through it all, to come out the other end a free woman. I was also so drained and tired, but desperate to get home to my partner.

When I arrived home, Val just dropped me off. I went into the house and collapsed into my husband's arms. He told me to lie down, and he made me a cup of tea and gave me a tranquillizer that the doctor had prescribed for me. I fell asleep. My phone was going mad with calls from family and friends wanting to know what had happened and if I was OK. My husband answered the calls and assured them I was all right.

The following day, later on, the procurator fiscal from the high court telephone me to tell me my brother had been found guilty and sentenced to eight years. I was thrilled at this news, as all I'd wanted was to be believed and I was now.

These two trials were over. I had the aftermath to deal with, still getting counselled, then referred on to the trauma team, as one of my counsellors said, also one of the police officers said, it was one of the worst paedophile ring cases they had ever heard of, and I also was told how strong I was to go through with it.

I know there are still predators out on the street, and I will do everything in my power to get these people behind bars too, as children are precious and should be protected. Some people ask why I left it so long. My answer is firstly because I feared for my life; they would have killed me, and thanks to my husband, my close brothers and my son, I'm still alive, and secondly, to get some sort of justice for that poor girl, Margaret Fleming, who was tortured and abused. I do also hope that they tell someone where they buried her body; the people and her remaining family have a right to know so Margaret can rest in peace.

As an adult survivor of childhood sexual abuse, I want awareness out there that children should speak out; it's not their fault, they are innocent.

A counsellor once said to me, "Sandra, a child should be able to dance around the home naked and no one should have any sick ideas at all about touching that kid inappropriately."

Someone has got to save the children and also let adults know that it doesn't matter what age you are, you can still let the secret of abuse out, as it is not healthy to keep inside the sickness that another human being planted in you. So I beg you, please tell someone, because if you have been abused and you keep it hidden, you will have major triggers your whole life.

I thought all men were child predators. If I went shopping and heard a child cry, I would automatically think that child had been abused. I had to get used to the words 'special girl', 'princess', 'my wee angel' and lots more, because when I hear men calling a child any of these names my trigger starts and I just assume that child is being abused. Even if a child bed wets, this doesn't mean sexual abuse. I had to learn all these things the hard way. So many people out there, men and women, are still suffering from child abuse and neglect.

I am a survivor today. I still have my music,

my singing, as my escape. I helped Police Scotland get two murderers and a master of a paedophile ring behind bars, and I am still working to get the others arrested. They have been questioned and, I assure you, Sandra will get her justice and closure on them all.

One of my aims for this book is to increase awareness and to assure you that, if you have been a victim of abuse or neglect, you can get help and you can find your freedom. The help is out there, just waiting for you to speak up and ask for support.

Today I have a comfortable life. I'm a very strong woman who is using her historical, childhood sexual abuse in a positive way, to keep awareness up that these monsters are still out there, and also to help the victims to stand together – there's strength in numbers – and be positive. Please don't let your coping medicine be alcohol or drugs, as they will kill you, the abuse won't, it will make you stronger and you can help so many other suffering victims break their silence. Breaking my silence definitely freed my soul of the bondage of past, historical sexual abuse. This applies to men and women, boys and girls who are victims of this most horrific crime.

I'm glad I broke my silence. I am now a very brave woman that can take these little Sandras out, nurture them, tell them they are safe and then tuck them back in, as these kids are all part of me. And you know what? I like me today. I do not drink alcohol, I do not take drugs, and I am blessed with being clean and not needing these toxins as a coping mechanism.

I do hope this book helps a lot of people, and I thank you all from the bottom of my heart for believing me. It's such a freedom to become:

A survivor
From a victim
RIP Margaret

Where to Get Help

Women's Aid

Rape Crisis

CIS'ters

NSPCC

National Association for People Abused in Childhood (NAPAC)

Police Scotland

Victim Support

Sandyford Clinic

Glasgow Trauma Team: The Anchor

NHS Scotland, England and Wales, and HSC Northern Ireland

Colin MacKillop, the best psychologist in Glasgow

There are many, many more worldwide organisations, just google it, the help is there.

Acknowledgements

A big thank you to all who believed in me and gave me the encouragement and strength to write my book:

My husband, big James McMenamin

My son and daughter

Jamie Son, my godson

My brothers, Joseph, Vincent and Edward

My family in Canada and Australia

Wee Richie, my best pal

Mandy Moore, for your time and patience with me

Helen McCall, for great guidance and support from the very start

And all my other trusted family and friends. I love you all dearly. I can forgive but, dear God, I can't forget. I just hope you find your inner voice, as I found mine.

Oh, thanks Pearl for being so close, like a sister she is.

I could go on and on, but you all know who you are that stood by me.

God bless
Keep safe
Keep on keeping on

Printed in Great Britain
by Amazon